The Religion of the Aryo-Germanic Folk

The Religion of the Aryo-Germanic Folk

Esoteric and Exoteric

Guido von List

Lodestar
P. O. Box 16
Bastrop, Texas 78602
USA

www.seekthemystery.com

This Book is Dedicated to one of the most noble women and mothers of the Aryo-Germanic Folk:

Mrs. Victorine Wannieck
in Munich
with
great reverence
by
the Author

Introduction

The intellectual world of Guido von List is a fascinating one. List lived and flourished in the heady atmosphere of *fin-de-sièle* Vienna— a seething cauldron of the human spirit our of which emerged ideas that would dominate the 20th century. List was primarily an artist— a poet. As a poet his medium was the *word*. He begins this treatise on "the Religion of the Aryo-Germanic Folk" with a meditation on the phrase: "In the beginning was the word..." Perhaps characteristic of List, he does not mention the more contextually profound Eddic take on the primacy of the word (Hávamál 141). Such oversights were common in List's work simply because the time was not right to discuss the Germanic tradition in such a pure manner. List's mystical world-view was in fact dominated by the doctrines of Theosophy with which he combined Germanic data. Many today see List as an intellectual forerunner, a pioneer, but think, in the spirit List himself puts forward, that we can do better today than he was able to do then. In this brief introduction I would like to address three major ideas: the use of folk-etymology as a mystical technique, Theosophy in List's ideology and the myth of of "Ariosophical" culpability in crimes committed by National Socialists. For a more comprehensive introduction to the ideology of Guido von Lit, see the introduction to my translation of *The Secret of the Runes* (Destiny, 1988).

Listian Folk-Etymology as Mystical Thought

One of List's more original contributions to the lore of mystical thought is his adaptation of Indian doctrines on the mystical contents of seed-words or syllables (*bijas*) to create a virtual mystical science of folk etymology for Germanic words. Folk-etymology is a common phenomenon. It is the attempt by nonscientific laymen to generate (often mythically tinged) origins of words or to show the meaningful connections between words based on the way they might sound alike. Folk etymology is responsible for people once believing that "wicca" had something to do with "wise," apparently simply because they both began with a "w." Folk etymologies are always easier to believe than actual etymologies derived from linguistic and philological data according to established rules of diachronic linguistics simply because they *appear* more plausible to the untrained eye. List took this idea one step deeper by concentrating not on the superficial level, but rather on words syllable by syllable. For example on page 37 of the present text he takes the Old Norse word *ljóssálfar*, which is actually a compound of the words for "light" (*ljóss*) and "elves" (*álfar*) and breaks it down in a mysto-syllabic manner: *lio* = light; *sal* = holiness; *far* = solar-generation, i.e. "salvation generated through light and the sun." In doing this he is not inventing a method out of whole cloth, but rather is following methods laid down by Indian mystics who analyze Sanskrit words in a similar metalinguistic manner. The result is a kind of mystical, suprarational understanding of language that is somewhat akin to the way in which kabbalistic mystics use number and numerical value to understand words on another level.

Theosophical Characteristics of List's Ideology

The Theosophical Society is a synthetic and syncretizing mystical school founded primarily by the Russian expatriate Helena Petrovna Blavatsky (née von Hahn) in New York City in 1875. It became established in German-speaking central Europe in subsequent years and influenced many esoteric schools there. However, it must be said that there was very little that was original about Theosophy. It was a synthesis of practically everything that had preceded it as far as mysticism and magic were concerned. It possessed an elaborate doctrine concerning the evolution of the races of humanity, and where this evolutionary process was headed. Again the ideas were not new or peculiar to Theosophy in 1875, but they did find a forceful vehicle in the works of Blavatsky, especially her voluminous *Secret Doctrine* (1888). Already on page 3 of the present work by List he outlines specifically Theosophical ideas on race: "...the Third Race of humans was still androgynous, and that only with the Fourth Race were the male and female genders split, which also continues to be the case in the Fifth Race— our own." On page 23 he presents the Theosophical theoretical idea about how more advanced racial souls are "awakened earlier than the others" and thereby gain power over relatively undeveloped souls. These concepts are essentially borrowed from Theosophy, using Theosophical terminology (e.g. "Root Races"). Doctrines of spiritual hierarchy are contained in the Germanic tradition, which can be discovered in the text of various Old Norse poems, e.g. the Rígsþula in the *Poetic Edda*. But the Germanic tradition can not be construed as being identical with that of Theosophy.

The Modern Myth of "Ariosophical" Culpability for Nazi Crimes

More than once my former work with the early 20th century rune-magicians and Guido von List has caused a critic or two to remark to the effect that I failed to point out that these esoteric ideas led directly to Auschwitz. One German academic Stephanie von Schnurbein writing in her *Religion als Kulturkritik* [(Winter, 1992) p. 136] remarked concerning my introduction to *The Secret of the Runes*: "*Dabei erwähnt [Flowers] an keine Stelle, daß List und die andere Ariosophen Vordenker des Rassenwahns des Nationalsozialismus waren...*" (In this work [Flowers] nowhere mentions that List and the other Ariosophists were intellectual predecessors of the racial madness of National Socialism...). It is just taken as a matter of course, with little to no actual critical investigation, that the ideas of List, Lanz and others were directly implemented in the Nazi genocide. A critical analysis would, however, show that such was not the case. First of all, no one has ever shown that racial policies of the NSDAP are based on so-called "Ariosophical" ideas. The very term "Ariosophy" points to its having been created as something based by analogy on its predecessor, Theosophy. All of the racal ideas contained in Ariosophy can be traced to Theosophy, and even the most "extreme" of the Ariosophists, Lanz von Liebenfels (cited several times by List in the present book) cannot be show to have been an Anti-Semite in any way comparable to the anti-Semitism practiced by the Nazis. Lanz not unfavorably about the Jews and cooperated with learned Jews in many of his publications. If individual Nazis became familiar with some of the mystical racism of Theosophy through the works of List and Lanz, this does not make the latter culpable in the crimes of the former. Why not blame Theosophy? Actually, of course, the Anti-Semitism that drove Nazi policies was much older and more deeply rooted in the people of central Europe than can be accounted for in a few fringe works by mystics and rune-magicians. The roots of Nazi anti-Semitism is in the Christian churches, both Catholic and Lutheran, but most especially the Catholic Church. It was the Catholic Church Fathers who first invented ideas about the Jews being an inferior "race," and who drove Anti-Semitic policies right up to and all during the Second World War. (See David Kertzer, *Popes Against the Jews* [Knopf, 2001].) The real truth about the "occult (= hidden) roots of Nazi Anti-Semitism" is that these roots are to be found in Christian doctrines and teachings, not in pagan Germanic ones. The postwar insistence upon the "occult" roots of these ideas is simply a matter of misdirecting historical attention away from the age-old perpetrator of the ideas and toward a "straw man" who is at present perceived as being too weak to defined himself. It is safe to blame "mystical sects" and "pagans" for the crimes in question because these folks are so few and so historically weak that they cannot defend themselves (nor are many even interested in "defending" themselves) and few others (even in the name of truth) will stand up to defend them for fear of being tarred with the same brush.

In any event, the works of Guido von List are interesting due to their spiritual rather than political content. Despite whatever weaknesses the works might be seen to have from today's perspective, they are most often worthy of our careful study. Pioneers and visionaries such as Guido von List represents remain the kind of men whose words we never tire of hearing.

A Note on Translating List

German writers in the Listian tradition, such as Wiligut, Marby and others, are notoriously difficult to translate due to their frequent use of puns and wordplays to illustrate their folk-etymlogical practices. Where it has been found necessary I have included the original German word in square brackets: [/]. There is additional editorial information which also appears enclosed in square brackets. This includes certain notes and commentaries as well as the frequent supply of an original German word where the philosophical content of that word might help those with some knowledge of German better understand the original thought behind the translation.

List is known for his incredibly long and often convoluted sentences, which are sometimes difficult to follow in German, but would create impossible English sentences if the translation always kept the sentences as long as the original. However, in this translation I have tried to retain as much of the original quality of List's style as possible.

Old Norse words are usually left in the form that List used, although the orthography he uses is obviously influenced by continental German usage.

> As Christianity was making its inroads,
> Heathenry did not cease; the old religion
> only disappeared in relation to the new
> one insofar as it had to yield in its public
> exercise of heathen practices, which in no
> way means that it also had to cease in its
> inner sense, in the characteristic life of the
> folk.
>
> Mone, Introduction to the *Nibelungenlied*

Until now much too much mythology and much too little religious study, much too much grammar and much too little linguistic study has been undertaken to be able to recognize that the impenetrable crystal bowl around which some people uselessly circle without ever being able to open it up, will practically open itself for anyone who understands how to use as a magical key the well-known, and yet so little understood, sentence: "In the beginning was the word."(1)

But the apparently mystical aspects of this statement immediately disappear, and we are transported into a full state of clarity, when it is realized that, without exception, all mythological names and other kinds of mythological terms were in no way mere empty words, but rather they signified quite specific concepts, and in these very meaningful terms the key to the knowledge and understanding of the religion of our ancient ancestors is offered. Additionally, remnants of customs, sayings, tales, etc., have maintained their meaning and value only through such recognition of the force of language contained in the mythical names and terms, so that linguistic and mythic research, in a complementary way, yield a sense of the sacrality of the word in a complete vindication of the phrase: "In the beginning was the word."

If then, in the beginning was the word (*language*) in which the feelings and knowledge of the human soul were expressed, then this language must have been so deeply bound to what is generally termed "religion" (which our ancient ancestors much more sensibly called *Wihinei*) that a division was, and is, impossible, and that therefore a conversion from one religion to another must have been just as impossible as splitting *Wihinei* off from language. And so it was in fact. The Christianization of the Aryo-Germanic folk was merely an outward one. While the *Wihinei* of the ancient ancestors, usually called heathens, even today still provides a form for the content of Christianity, which only outwardly differentiates itself from Wuotanism, and even this only superficially. This was because those who converted the heathens were unable to create any other language. And so Christian concepts — in order to be made intelligible — had to be designated with familiar heathen names created from the language of *Wihinei*. Certainly they had attempted to Latinize the Germanic language for this purpose, but it remained only an attempt, as the Germanic folk would not allow their language to be stolen from them. But due to this attempt they were driven by necessity to reach back to the old holy language of the heathen *Wihinei* to derive, and form from it, their own mystery-language. How this happened is to be discussed in more detail in one of the next volumes of our series. [This would be *Die Ursprache der Ario-Germanen und ihre Mysteriensprache*, ed.]

From what we have said it is easy to see that the original Aryo-Germanic language was, and remained, the holy secret language, which was taken into the "high secret tribunal" [*hohe heimliche Acht*] by the men of knowledge— the *Armanen*(2) or *Semanen*. As a result of this the primeval language remained almost unchanged through millennia, while the popular languages which were based on it, and developed out of it, became more and more distinct from it in a steady change, so that finally the holy, or secret, language (mystery-language) was no longer understood by the uninitiated (profane persons), although it was common knowledge in primeval times.

The obvious result of the progressive disintegration of the folk-languages from the holy primeval — and now secret — language was also the split of the old *Wihinei* into two different teachings. These were the secret doctrine belonging to those of knowledge (esotericism), which is here to be called "Armanism" for the sake of brevity, and into the general religious doctrine of the people (exotericism), which for the sake of easier understanding will be termed "Wuotanism." The point at which Wuotanism began to branch off from Armanism is to be discovered where the brief characteristic terms for the highest incomprehensible and unfathomable divine essence were no longer understood by the uninitiated, so that they were reduced to individual names in such a way that eventually an anthropomorphic entity (personality) bearing a name, was created out of the great incomprehensible divine essence. These individual characteristics were further anthropomorphized (given human shape) such that they formed a series of gods, which, becoming ever more human, arranged themselves like a great royal family around a high-king until eventually even the familial relationships were no longer sufficient and the ranks of servants in all their hierarchies had to be instituted to complete the picture for the lower divinities.

This rise of the different anthropomorphized divine entities of Wuotanism out of the equally manifold terminology for the characteristics of the incomprehensible One of Armanism was in no way the first step toward the branching off of the popular doctrine from the secret doctrine, but rather the third such branching off. For the first step toward dividing the two doctrines was the designation of the first sexless (androgynous, not hermaphroditic) divinity as man-wife, which is self-regenerating. The second step toward division characterizes that section of the mythologies in which feminine divinities, "the virginal mothers of the gods," are named as primal divinities who are able to bear the son of a god without sexual means.

But those characteristic designations of the unfathomable One, as well as the anthropomorphized divine entities which originated from them are neither arbitrary nor accidentally generated, but rather they are based upon primeval calendrical observations of the countless gradations of kind and out of the transitions between night and day, darkness and light, cold and warmth, as well as those developed out of the rotational periods of the Sun, Moon and planets, by which the gods of time came into view alongside those of space. The personal as well as celebratory names of these gods are, however, again manifested in the light of the secret mystery-language in simple, yet definite, signs of the ruling divine forces in the cycle of the ring of the year.

Thus we see that in the course of countless millennia (the more exact calculation of which will be further explained later in this book), from the original beginnings of the Aryan race, the holy original language determined what sorts of things based on the intuitive knowledge concerning the evolution of all being needed to the brought into pragmatic expression. Therefore we see this original language as a holy secret language within the high secret tribunal of Armanendom and something truly preserved with it as a high-holy tradition, which has been maintained as a secret doctrine right up to our time in the form of Armanism. Thus we finally just see this very holy secret language as Armanism craftily concealed in the *Wihinei* of Wuotanism as if enclosed in that precious crystal bowl which can only be opened with the magical key of that well-known, yet seldom understood, formula: "In the beginning was the word."

It was then from that threefold division, or better said from that three-leveled classification, of the idea of divinity conceived of in Wuotanism, which portrayed the primal-god [*Urgott*] androgynously, i.e. double-sexed, that the primal-mother [*Urmutter*] emerged, only after which the long series of older and younger divinities, of masculine and feminine gender arose. Only in passing it may be mentioned that this three-leveled classification is neither fable nor metaphor, but actual fact which, of course, encompasses a space of time of millions of years. Concerning this we can only go so far as to say that the Third Race of humans was still androgynous, and that only with the Fourth Race were the male and female genders split, which also continues to be the case in the Fifth Race— our own. These are merely the dim recollections of the human soul such as find expression in old mythical documents, but which belong to an entirely different field of investigation than the one we are pursuing here, and therefore we will say nothing further of them here.

That primal mystery is expressed in the high mythical song of the *Edda*, the "Völuspá" as follows:

> In the primal beginnings Ymir lived there
> As yet there was no sand, nor sea, nor wind
> No earth down below, nor heaven up above—
> Yawning emptiness, nowhere did the grass grow.

Yawning emptiness — primal abyss — chaos — *Ginnungagap*! This is what modern science calls the primeval fog [*Urnebel*], that is the original Element out of which all the modern elements radiate.

Above that yawning void of the abyss, an immeasurable self-contained force hovers latently, an unmoved mover, an impersonal cause which can be called the "hidden God," which is to be considered the impersonal, immaterial spirit that is within itself both time and space. By means of his breath he condensed himself into matter,(3) which he has himself now become, but without himself ceasing to be— and so spirit and matter, energy and matter, are indivisibly One. Until that distant end in which matter once more dissolves and becomes non-physical and spiritual. Therefore spirit is eternal and is immutable Being. As solidified spirit it is eternal, for it is one with this spirit. At the moment of the condensation of spirit into *prima materia*, or the original element— or as others express it with other words: "as spirit radiantly flowed into matter" (Let there be light), the previously hidden, still unrevealed God revealed himself as the First Logos. This original element then developed into the first four elements: fire (Muspellsheim), water (Audhumbla), air (Niflheim), and earth (Ymir). Three other elements — which remain unknown to us – developed at the same time, and only the fifth element, ether or aether, can be recognized at this time. Knowledge of the sixth and seventh elements is reserved to the future Sixth and Seventh Races.

The element of earth— embodied in Ymir — is now being evolved further in its own right. The giant Ymir, it is said, fell asleep and thereupon his left foot engendered a son with his right foot. This son is the patriarch of the giants. At the same time the element of water, the cow Adhumbla, licked out of the salt-stone a man named Buri, who was also double-sexed (androgynous) and by himself he engendered a son named Bör, who then had three sons with the names Wuotan, Wili and We with a daughter of the giant Bergthor of Ymir's family. These three sons of Bör slew the giant Ymir, drug his body out into the empty space between Muspellsheim (fire) and Niflheim (air) and shaped out of him that which we call our world.

> From Ymir's flesh was the earth created
> From his sweat (blood) the sea,
> From his bones the mountains, the trees from his hair
> From his skull heaven,
> From his eyebrows the gracious Ases created
> Midgard for the sons of men,
> But from his brain are formed
> All the hardhearted clouds.
>
> Grímnismál [41-42]

But on the occasion of Ymir's murder there flowed so much blood that the entire race of rime-giants drowned in it, except for one named Bergalmir (Bergalt = mountain-old), whose father was named Thrud-gelmir (*Starkalt* = strong-old) and his grandfather Oergelmir (*Uralt* = extremely old, i.e. Ymir).(4) This Bergelmir saved himself and his family from the flood in a "cradle" that he used as a boat. In the earthly world that was formed after this flood, he propagated the giant-race further, where the dwelling places were shown to the younger giant-race on the other side of the world-sea surrounding the future dwelling place of the coming human race— Midgard, that is, Arktegea, the land around the North-Pole, which was the place of the origin of the Aryans.

But even before humans came to the earth, the human fortress [Menschenburg] that had been prepared for them was animated by the dwarves who had earlier evolved from mere worms and maggots in the dead body of Ymir, but later they received from the gods human shape and human intelligence, but no human soul— and they lived in dark caves and rock crevices. Ymir's skull arched over the earth as the heavenly sky, at the four ends of which the gods placed four dwarves as conductors of the major winds: Austri, Vestri, Sudri and Nordri. Then they took the sparks and lights that had flown out of Muspellsheim, placed them in the sky in order to illuminate both it and the earth. They assigned each of these fiery sparks its place, and in so doing they fixed some of them in the sky, while others were allowed to run free, but even these had their orbits determined and were ordered in their courses according to space and time and thus originated day and night and the enumeration of the years.

In this way the earth had been prepared for humanity. All of creation with the exception of humans had been completed, but in this stage of completion its further evolution was also prefigured. Thus the primeval age came to an end.

As obscure and vague as the figures of Ymir, Audhumbla, Buri and Bör might appear, they nevertheless cast their reflections rather plainly out of the primeval age of humanity over into the days of our Fifth Race and tell with vigorous characteristics about times long ago separated from the people of today by millions of years. But Ymir has to be viewed from two different perspectives. First, from the standpoint of Armanism he is something impersonal, i.e. the primeval matter of fixed earth that evolved out of the primeval mist [Urelement]. Second, from the standpoint of Wuotanism, he is viewed as the personification of the primitive races which in ancient times preceded our Fifth Root Race, and which were brought to an end by the deluge (the Deucalionian Flood).

Only with the appearance of the first divine triad is the Second Logos revealed and then the division of divinity into three and then seven forces, or characteristics, begins. These forces appear in humanized forms as the Ases or gods.

The Ases — in the literal sense the "pillars of the world" — create the earth, seas, the sky, the entire visible world out of the slain Ymir, the "primeval element," but not human beings as such— only their outer forms as Ask and Embla. It is only Wuotan himself who gifts them with spirit and soul, after Lodur gave them blood and blooming hue [body] and Hœnir gave them sense (intellect, mind). And this is very meaningful!

The oldest divine triad to be named is: "Wuotan, Wili, We," later they are called "Wuotan, Hœnir, Lodur," and then "Wutoan, Donar Freyr," or "Wuotan, Donar, Fricco"— and in the Younger Edda they appear once as "Har, Jafnhar, Thridi." Wuotan or Odin is always the

First One and his name remains unaltered, while the Second and Third change their names. Even more telling is the third triad: "Har, Jafnhar, Thridi," which literally means: "the High One (Har = Ar = Sun, Right, the High, etc.), the "Just-As-High," and the Turner (*trie* = to turn [*drehen*], to wind, not "the third"). The Ases can only shape the form of humanity, and only Wuotan provides humanity with spirit, the human soul, while Hœnir conveys the lower soul or intellect, and Lodur gives the material body. The name Wuotan or Odhin (Od-in = spirit within), however, indicates that its bearer is the most powerful of the three, and that he himself is actually the One and Only. But this singular One is actually the second manifestation of the divine spirit revealing itself through materialization. He is the Second Logos, and as such he is the "All-Father," who can be portrayed in a human form superimposed over Wuotan, while he can also appear in human form as Wuotan himself. All-Father, who is also called Surtur (the Dark-One, not the Black-one), as his name indicates, is the All-creator and Wuotan is his reflection in human form, and as such Wuotan is also rightfully called the "All-Father— for he is "One with his Father in Heaven."

That which concerns the essence of the Triad of Gods as such symbolizes the three stages: "coming into being — becoming — and passing away (toward new arising)," and this is expressed by all groups of names in all mythical triads. These always symbolize the same triad in various aspects, whether or not these begin with Wuotan as the first element, e.g. the Nornic triad: "Urda, Verdandi, Skuld." Urda means: That which has been there from the beginning, thus that which has come into being; Verdandi is that which is becoming; and Skuld is the effect and cause of becoming, in either the good or bad sense according to circumstances.

And likewise all other names in various triads speak in exactly the same symbolic way. For example, "Wuotan" = spirit-within, or spiritual action, the thinker, breath. "Wili" = *uil-li* = spiritual light = will; Hœnir [Hâner] = *han, an* = knowing [*ahnen*], the knower; Donar = *tun-ar* = the highly or rightly doing-one; "Lodur" = primal fire; "Loki" = fire-mighty; "Freyr" = the destroyer; "Fricco" = ruler of death. So again in these triads we see arising, becoming and passing away toward new arising. Designations of certain abstract characteristics in Armanism merely become divine proper names in Wuotanism. As Har, Jafnhar and Thridi appear as the High-One, Equally-High and the Turner or Transformer (not Ender). All three are, however, One in the All-Father, the Creator of All. This also emerges from the name of the famous temple of the Triad of Gods: Wuotan, Donar, Fricco which was called "Upsalar" (see Uppsala in Sweden), and in the high secret interpretation *up-sal*, i.e. highest salvation, indicates the All-Father. Many other place-names spread all throughout Germany and throughout all of Europe and beyond, all one-time sanctuaries of those divine triads, could be named here, but a few examples should suffice for our purposes: Sol-are = Zuolare = Solre = Zollern = "Hohenzollern" = High Rulership of the Sun or High Solar Salvation. Triglav = threefold life or arising life (the name is proto-Aryo-Germanic and not Slavic). Trier = Triur = arising from the primeval state [*Ur*]. Gibraltar = *gibor-altar* = giver, generator of all, i.e. the providing All-Father. (This has nothing to do with Arabic *gibel tarik*). *Götterweig* = Kotwig = God-hallowed [*Gottgeweiht*]. And still countless other names.(5)

A similar triad is that of the Norns (*nor*-stone, the fixed, foundational and non-born, originated), who indicate another revelation of the Second Logos, as in the *Edda* they are also called the unborn ones, i.e. the causeless cause, like the divine triad Wuotan-Wili-We. It has already been said that they indicate arising, becoming and passing away toward a new arising. However, this is not arbitrarily applied to the life of entities, but rather to their destiny. And this too relates to the name of the "Germans" in the most intimate way.

Garma is destiny *gar* = to ferment [*gähren*] **to be transformed into one's self**, to *germ*inate; thus *germ* = the yeast (from *hevan* = to rise through fermentation), to weld [*gärben*], to be refined [*gar sein*], etc. *ma* = more, make. Garma (Sanskrit *karma*) = **"making one's self transform within one's self, by means of one's self,"** i.e. one's own commissions and omissions, as causes, generate from themselves and by means of themselves effects, and these effects constitute Garma (*karma*) or destiny. Since there is only one "causeless cause," i.e. God, this first causeless cause as it relates to Garma or destiny is the oldest Norn, Urda, who has been there [*da*] from the beginning [*Ur*]. The second Norn is evolving Garma (Verdandi) and the third Norn— the dark (not black!) one is Skuld [*Schuld* = debt, guilt]. If our deeds of commission and omission were good, and something which led to transformation then good credit accrues; if it was bad then debt accrues. But because this debt is only payable in the future, it is considered to be dark, or hidden, and only perceptive can lift the veil (Image of Saïs) and happy is he for whom conscience — his own judge! — lifts the veil of Skuld.

This knowledge-based faith, free of any doubt, in the self-created and self-creating Garma (destiny) which has human beings in its power, and which is no "blind fate," no "doom," was so firmly rooted in the convictions of our heathen forefathers that they referred to themselves as those with power over destiny, the "*Garmanen*," or "Germans." This was recognized as early as Johannes Aveneius (Thurmayr 1477-1534), who correctly derived the tribal name "*Germanen*" from *germinare* = to sprout forth," even if he did not interpret it quite correctly.

In the two mythical names Sunilgarm and Munilgarm, the solar-wolf and the lunar-wolf respectively, this *garm* appears once again with this meaning, for both wolves, or dogs, are actually the kin of these heavenly bodies, or their destinies.

All of the mystical and mythical triads have not yet been named, not by a long shot, but it should suffice here to mention that all of them refer to that conceptual realm which they serve to symbolize, and this will quite often be referred to throughout this monograph.

With the first divine triad, however, the division emerged between the masculine and feminine essences with regard to anthropomorphized divinity. In the very beginning these apparently arose independently alongside one another (Ymir : Adhumbla; Wuotan, Wili, We : Urda, Verdandi, Skuld), but they soon appeared joined in matrimonial arrange-

8

ments, which mutually completed and explained them. About this more later. But it is not only as wives or brides that the goddesses stand beside the gods, but rather they often appear in noteworthy correlations which most certainly developed from primeval bisexual (androgynous) godforms. Thus, just to emphasize a twofold example, the Sun — *sol* — is feminine, but possesses a solar god — Freyr or Frô — who conversely had a priestess; while the Moon — *mani* — is thought of as masculine, but has a goddess — Freya — who is served by a sacrificial priest. The day, which rules the Sun, is masculine — Dag, Dellinger — and the night, ruled by the Moon is anthropomorphicized in feminine form—Nott. All of these gods and goddesses, however, had their spouses as well as descendants, through whom quite noteworthy familial relationships developed. According to their names these can easily be explained as children of the Sun or Moon (descendants of the day or night) and show that originally these gods were considered bisexual (androgynous), and only in more recent times had they been sexually divided in order to fit in with the rest of the divine world. Thus even the most recent anthropomorphicizations of divine ideas are consistently rooted, directly or indirectly, in the very oldest mystical and mythical concepts, as will be repeatedly demonstrated in this study.

Once the division of the One-god into the Tri-dvinity within the graded system of arising, becoming and passing away toward a new arising has been recognized, their breakdown into the "sevenfold-divinity" can be demonstrated in what follows. Because the white light of the Sun is split up through the prism into the seven-leveled spectrum of the rainbow, and because tones rise along seven levels toward a higher octave, and because the seven-leveled vibratory law governing everything else, down to asserting itself in the equivalencies of atomic weights, such that this seven-leveled vibratory law regulates the entire organism of the universe — such that anyone who grasps this vibratory law, and who completely understands how to use it, can claim the universal power of God for himself — it then immediately becomes clear what deep knowledge of the hidden forces of nature led to the divinization of that heptad, in that the unity was dissolved into a heptad, just like sun-light is broken up into the seven rays of the prism. The very word "seven" is holy in the language of the holy *Acht*, it means "sun," and to swear by seven [*besiebenen*] means to swear by the Sun. For this reason the Seven-Gods were the most holy, their cooperation became the "harmony of the spheres" and as all of them were unified in the One All-Father who is the primeval fire (*Urfyr*), likewise this One was dissolved into Seven, which it is in itself. Armanism knew this vibratory law well and with it pressed deeply into the most secret mysteries of the universe and of divinity. But this knowledge was only cultivated by the most qualified — and even today this is so — which is proven out by many experiences and traditions often ridiculed by modern science as superstition, yet proven to be valid through progressive discoveries in the areas of physics and chemistry, which are nevertheless provided with the new nomenclature for of fear of the "high holy tribunal," and "metaphysics"— allowances had to be made and the errors of the so-called exact sciences had to be admitted to.

However, it is not our assignment to follow the tracks of metaphysics, as tempting as this might be, but nevertheless this reference should suffice to show that ***Wihinei*** ["religion"] **and science are one, and that these apparently irreconcilable opposites will in the foreseeable future again become one, because they must be one.** Then humans can once more be happy because they must be happy — out of duty toward happiness, out of duty toward harmony, out of duty toward beauty!

These Seven-Gods, as the holiest, received their assigned heavenly bodies as their mystical residences and are still today designated as the planetary spirits in what is misunderstood as "astrology," and according to which the seven-day week is arranged and the days named. These seven planets are: 1. the Sun ☉, 2. Moon ☾, 3. Mars ♂, 4. Mercury ☿, 5. Jupiter ♃, 6. Venus ♀, and 7. Saturn ♄. This arrangement and designation, still in general use today, are not without good reason taken as a starting point here since they are only apparently at variance with the Armanic and Wuotanistic arrangement when it comes to nomenclature, but in spite of this they correspond perfectly to the Armanic system and therefore greatly ease our understanding of the latter. In the Sun, in the primeval fire [*Urfyr*], the All-Father can be recognized. The sign of the empty circle ○ is *Ur*, the unrevealed God, while the sign of the circle with the point in the middle ☉ designates God revealed in matter (First Logos). ☉ is therefore not the Sun as such, but rather it is the God revealed as the First Logos, as Father-Mother and as All-Father, merely whose symbol is the Sun. For this reason the high holy *Acht* has two signs for it: ☉ for the Sun as such and ◉ for the spiritual Sun, the primeval fire [*Urfyr*], God, or All-Father; in secret scriptures it is also called *psychhelia*. (This was because at certain times it was thought that without the use of foreign words this name could not be pronounced— or that it needed to be hidden.) The Moon ☾ was *mani* or Mannus, the progenitor of humanity, which once more forms a special section in the [Blavatsky's] *Secret Doctrine*. It has already been said above that the Ases could only create the bodies of humans and their lower soul, the intellect, and only Wuotan — as All-Father (he who is one with his father in heaven) — could give them the *divine* human soul. Now, the *Secret Doctrine* says that the Moon was the father of the Earth, and in a state of torpor — much like that of death — it shriveled up and became smaller than the Earth and was forced to follow alomg in the orbit of the Earth as its satellite, and it gave up its developed inhabitants to the Earth and these form the race of men here on the Earth in contrast to those formed from the earthly animal kingdom. These spirits descended from the Moon — the lunar ancestors — whom the All-Father incarnated into the bodies of those created by the other two Ases (Hœnir and Lodur) to form the human race, and for this reason Mannus, the Moon, is called the progenitor of humanity. Here too there are two signs, i.e. ☾ for the Moon itself and ☽ for Mannus or Mene, the spiritual Moon (Psychomena). The third, Mars ♂ is Tyr, Zio, also Zeizzo or Erich, the one-armed sword-god, the "generator." His hieroglyph also consists of the sign of *Ur* ○ and the Tyr-rune ↑, which symbolizes the solar ray, the solar arrow as impregnator (phallus). His sword, his one-arm , his *phallus ererctus*, clearly designates him as the provider of increase, the multiplier or generator under whose guardianship marriages stood, but war as well, since war increased property through the taking of booty and drove out vermin. The fourth, Mercury ☿ , is Wuotan, whose rune (*othil* ᛟ) is in this instance reversed ᛟ and connected to the sign of increase + to form ☿, indicating the increaser, bringer of luck, the wish-god. But the hieroglyph of the bull ᛟ, which appears here combined with the sign of increase +, already in itself consists of the *Ur*-sign ○ combined with the hieroglyph of the Moon (Mannus) ᵕ, and means primeval generation, or "the one who generates things out of the *Ur*"; for this reason the same sign is to be found once more in the Zodiac as that of the bull (Taurus) or the primeval generator. That the ancients already thought of Wuotan as being essentially the same as Mercury or Hermes is shown in the writings of Cornelius Tacitus, Julius Caesar, *et al*. It is also no accident that Mercury is the planet closest to the Sun. The fifth of those high-holy Seven-Gods is Jupiter ♃, the Aryo-Germanic Thor (Donar). His hieroglyphic, however, *intentionally* distorted from the *fyrfos* 卐 just like the *gibor*-rune ᚷ, which represents this holy sign. The *fyrfos* (swastika) as the "Hammer of Thor" was one of the holiest secret signs of the high secret tribunal [*Acht*], and was intentionally concealed by the *Armanen* for purposes of Wuotanism at public religious services as shown only in an imperfect form. The secret sign of Wuotan, the *tryfos* or *wilfos*: ᛦ or ᛋ was kept absolutely secret and was not revealed to the folk even in the imperfect form. In place of it we find the othil-rune ᛟ or ☿ . The hieroglyph of Jupiter ♃, the *gibor*-rune ᚷ and ultimately the concealed holy-sign + of the *fyrfos* symbolize the high-holy crossed lightning bolts, which we recognize as the bundle of lightning bolts held in the raised right hand of Jupiter, just like the hammer Malmer (Mjölnir) that Thor carries. The sixth of the Seven-Gods emphasizes the sexual aspect as the connection to the *Ur*-word *sex* shows. Its holy-sign, consisting of increase + our of the *Ur* ○, already indicates this. It is this Venus ♀ , whose hieroglyph comes closest to that of Mercury clearly showing the close relationship between the two. As Mercury-Wuotan ☿ means "he who generates out of *Ur*," so too can Venus-Freya ♀ be seen as "she who bears forth out of *Ur*," as that "god-bearing virgin," whom we will once more meet with in the Zodiac as the constellation of Virgo, or just as we did with the *Ur*-generator and the constellation of Taurus. Just as he is the *Ur*-father, she is the *Ur*-mother, and therefore the two are unified as the divine royal couple. The Latin name Venus also corresponds perfectly to the Aryo-Germanic Freya, Fenus, Fenussin, since the mystery language is the Aryan proto-language itself in which Latin, Greek, Sanskrit, etc., are rooted, and thus all mythological names and concepts can be interpreted by means of this language. The last, the seventh of the Seven-Gods, is Saturn ♄ . The name consists of the two *Ur*-words: *sâ* = "generate" and *turn* = "turn," i.e. to cause something to stop, and therefore is the equivalent of death, or passing away, or transformation toward a new arising. This name Saturn, like so many other mythological names, is only a functional characterization which became the name of an

11

anthropomorphized elaboration of a divine essence. In the understanding of Armanism it is, however, a circumlocution for Surtur (Satur) and means "continually in the *Ur*," i.e. in the eternal. Through the portal of birth, in coming into being, a human encounters things such as essence, objects, events, times, etc.

Thus we have the course of becoming, life in our world of the senses, which allows us to leave this world through the gate of death— by dying once more, and to be prepared in the *Ur* for a renewed arising, for rebirth. The Arman calls this preparation in the *Ur* for the next rebirth or incarnation "Surtur," and for this reason God, or the All-Father prior to his materialization, is called "Surtur," and bears, after his dematerialization at the end of times, the same name— "Surtur." Even in the Christian Middle Ages the state of the soul in death was called the "primeval state" [*Urständ*], i.e. the condition within *Ur*. Therefore the hieroglyph of Saturn (Surtur) is the sign of increase + together with the *sal*-rune ⚡ or ⚡ , meaning an increase in salvation. Throughout the transformations which condition this passing away toward new arising (through dying and overcoming death for re-incarnation) it is just these reserves for salvation slumbering in the *Ur* which are released, and thus the soul, tarrying in the "primeval state," is able, depending to its own abilities, to develop and provide for its next incarnation on earth, and with these means to assimilate as many of the qualities from the treasury of such qualities stored in this state as it can. For this reason the god of death is no enemy of man, but rather his friend, who provides him with rich gifts during his stay in the "primeval state," for his next earthly life in a renewed human existence, in order to maintain the steady progress of the whole of humanity in an indefatigable process by means of these gifts. By concluding in "Surtur," or Saturn, the Seven have reached their end, only to begin the circulation once more from the beginning in the *Acht* (octave), but as with music on an *Acht* (octave) higher. Therefore the circulations do not take place on a horizontal plane, but rather in a spiral toward a definite goal, exactly as the planets in their orbits around the Sun — proceeding onward with the Sun in their collective course — rushing through unmeasured distances toward a goal which remains unknown to us.

Here it may be remembered that the seven colors of the rainbow, or spectrum, are really only three colors (blue, yellow and red) while the other colors are actually transitional tones. In a similar fashion we also clearly and precisely see in the Seven-Gods: the *Ur*-Three shining above the other four, which in a certain sense make the transitional tones between the Three recognizable. We will come back to this 3+4 and 3+7 in more detail when the opportunity is offered in our discussion of numerical symbolism.

It is quite obvious that there were other heptads in the Aryo-Germanic *Wihinei*, and, by way of example, we could just mention the seven goddesses of love, who are also known as the "Good Seven." They are ordered as follows:

Gefion (She who Gives), a virgin in fresh bloom. She gifts the children when they come into bloom as virgins with the honeydew of their pleasing essences, which have the power to coerce a man into love, and she also gathers all those into her entourage who die while still virgins, so that they can be escorted by her to new luck in love with renewed charms in their next incarnation.

Snotra is gifted with feminine grace and the charm of eloquent speech. She is the messenger of love in the service of Freya in that she puts thoughts of love into the hearts of lovers desired by others and shows them dream images of those who love them while they sleep.

Siofna fans Snortra's spark of love into a blazing flame in which the hearts of the lovers are melded into one, or if kept apart, each will wither.

Loba moves the maiden to give her chosen one the ring of Loba (an engagement ring [*Verlobungsring*]) under Loba's protection.(6)

Wara protects with flaming runes the oaths of fidelity in the hearts of lovers, and avenges the violation of these oaths.

Syna, she who is prudent, guards the lock on the door of the bridal chamber and avenges the crime of unallowed sexual pleasure. It is also she, the Sixth (sex, sexual) who opens the bridal chamber for the Seventh, the Sunny, for Lady Fene or Fane (the generative, birth-giving one, from whom we get our woman's name "Fanny," which has nothing to do with "Francesca"— although this is often erroneously thought to be the case). With her all of the joys of love and marriage enter into life and none is more modest in this regard than Freya herself— our chaste Aryo-Germanic *Venus genetrix*.

These "Good Seven" are contrasted with the "Evil Seven," whose names do not appear to have been recorded anywhere. But probably those "Evil Seven" are later distortions from the time of transition from Wuotanism to Christianity, a theme to which one of our next volumes will be devoted. [= *Der Übergang vom Wuotanismus zum Christentum*]

Our seven-day week is also derived from the "Seven Gods," and we only need a little help in order to grasp the meanings of the names immediately. Sunday and Monday do not require much further interpretation, since the Sun is seen as a symbol of the All-Father and the Moon (*man, mene, mannus*) is seen as a symbol of the lunar ancestors of terrestrial humanity, personified in the form of Mannus as the progenitor of all of humanity. The name *Dienstag* (Thiusdag), Erichtag (Irtag), Zistag, etc., relates to Thyr, Zio, Zeizzo, and Erich. *Mittwoch* [Wednesday] is merely an obfuscation of *Godestag* (Westphalian), *Odhinsdagr* (Norse) and therefore also needs no special explanation, just as *Donnerstag* [Thursday] and *Freitag* [Friday]. Old Norse *Friadagr* need none. Only *Samstag* [Saturday] causes some difficulties. The English, Frisians, Dutch and Lower Saxons left its actual name as *dies Saturni*: Sätensdäg, Säternsdäg, Saturday, Saterday, Saterdag, Satersdag; the Irish call it *dia Satuirn*, Satarn, the French *Samedi*, the Spanish *Sabado* and the Italians *Sabato*. But there is no German *Satarnes* or *Sazarnestag* — as it would have to appear — although there is a *Sambatstac* along with *Samestac* and a Gothic *Sabatodag* and *Sabbatus*. However, among all of these names the form *Sameztac* appears quite conspicuous. This word-form is derived from *sa-mezz* (*sa* = to make; *mezz* = to divide cut off: *Steinmetz* [stone-cutter] who chisels off stones— i.e. the day dividing the week) and indicates the transitional time from one week to another, which has the same meaning as *sa-turn* (to make turn) or *Sat-ur* (constantly in the *Ur*, i.e. rooted in the *Ur* and leading back to there) and finally even as *Surtur* (*sur-tur* = from *Ur* back to *Ur*).

With these Seven-Gods the divinities can be shown to be gods of time and as such they can be found even more clearly in the Twelve- and Thirteen-Gods. Certainly it does not again have to be recalled that Armanism simply names the expressions of power of the revealed One divinity through characterizations of its qualities, and that Wuotanism personified these names and took these essential qualities and interpreted them as divinized, yet anthropomorphic, entities. The Twelve- and Thirteen-Gods correspond to the months of the year, initially the thirteen lunar months, then later the twelve solar months. But since with this calendrical transition of the lunar year into the solar year the thirteenth month-god dropped out, i.e. symbolically died, this is how the aversion to the number thirteen arose, an aversion which holds that if thirteen people sit at a table one of them will have to die within the year. But which one of the thirteen is the one destined to die remains the choice of the divinity, which constantly selects its own sacrifice. And this election of the victim of the divinity is — and this only has to be mentioned parenthetically — the rationale underlying trial by ordeal, as well as games of chance (cards, dice, betting, etc.), duels and the lottery. But in no way did this idea lead to a belief, as is erroneously assumed, in fate ruling blindly, but rather it led to a consistent trust in a conscious divine course of destiny and its higher compensatory justice.

These twelve are also One, as it demonstrated by the fact that Wuotan, as the god of time or god of the year, bears a special name in each of the twelve months. These are:

1. *Hartung*, January: All-Father. The first month in the year is the highest, as All-Father is the first and highest of all the gods (cf. Sunday ☉ and ☉). From this first month all the subsequent months emerge, just as all the gods come from All-Father. The year begins with the longest night, and just as the Night — as a feminine entity — is thought of as the Mother of all things, the longest of nights — the "Great Mothernight," the "Holy-Night" — was the mother of the year.

2. *Hornung*, February: Herian = Army-Father, Army-God (not Lord-God [*Herrgott*]. Wuotan as the Sun (Exalted, Ar ☉), *Urfyr* (primeval fire) appears as the warrior (Herier) against Darkness, i.e. the rime- and frost-giants.

3. *Lenzmond*, March: Nikar = The victorious primeval light [*Urlicht*] which decides every battle; at the end of the month the days are already becoming longer than the nights.

4. *Ostermond*, April: Hnikudr = He who Overcomes. The giants are overcome, the Sun climbs ever higher.

5. *Mai*, May: Fiolnir = The Manifold. Life springs forth in manifold forms from the earth, now freed from the ice.

6. *Bracht, Brachet*,(7) June : Oski = He who has divine abilities, the gifts of God flow forth in rich abundance over the entire earth.

7. *Heuet*, July: Omi(8) = "the holy one who is praised. Everywhere jubilation and joy; the festival of summer.

8. *Aust*, August: Biflindi = "the one who is about to sink, the inconstant." The Sun is already beginning to sink (the white god of the sword is faltering).

9. *Scheiding*, September: Vidrir = "the weatherer," but also the generator of law" (*vid* = law, *rir* = to generate). The equinox with its stormy weather.

10. *Gilbhard*, October: Svidrir = "the disappearance of generated fruits." The fields are empty, the leaves turn yellow, and growth ceases.

11. *Laubris*, November: Svidur = "disappearing into the *Ur*." Storms rip leaves from the trees, whatever fruits remain outside will freeze.

12. *Wihimanoth*, *Julmonat*, December: Jalkr = "he who has died off." Snow covers the earth like silver hair covers the head of an elder.

Even if the One-God is still clearly recognizable in this Twelve-God system, its differentiated month-names soon began to take on the form of independent entities, which, according to a basic principle of mythology, are seen as his sons or other descendants. Each of these twelve month-gods possesses a fortress— a solar house. Here it is self-evident that these twelve fortresses are the twelve constellations or solar houses of the Zodiac. The coming together of the ancient correspondences of the Zodiac demonstrate the connections among all original religions, down to making their descent from Aryan *Wihinei* irrefutable. But because a deeper exploration of the Zodiac and it interconnections is impossible in these pages due to a shortage of space, only simple indications can be offered here. Perhaps later there will be a more fitting opportunity to come back to this topic. It is obvious that All-Father is reflected in every month-god and in every characteristic indicated by his specific month-name, and that Wuotan migrates through the twelve solar fortresses during the course of a year in the form of visitations which he holds with the various month-gods each in his or her own fortress.

These twelve month-gods and their fortresses are:

1. Hartung, January, Aquarius or Urn ♒: Freyr (Frô in Alfheim [elf-world]. The new-born Sun rules, the days are bright even if they are still short. All-Father and the gods celebrate the festival of the first tooth of Freyr (of the first ray of the Sun) of the newborn son of the Sun; humans celebrate Yule [*Weihnacht* = holy-night], New Year.

2. Hornung, February, Pisces ♓: Wal-Father (Wuotan as the one who conducts the dead to reincarnation) in Walaskialf (hall of the dead, Walhalla). Wuotan gathers to himself the "half of the Wal" (half of the dead[9]) which belongs to him, i.e. the souls which have lost their bodies, in Walaskialf, in order to conduct them toward reincarnation, i.e. up out of the "primeval state [*Urständ*] (Underworld) into the world of humans once more. It is just these souls, separated from their bodies, who are his army, which he victoriously leads against the forces of death — the rime- and frost-giants — and by means of which he overcomes death in that he awakens the dead to a new life through reincarnation. Humans celebrate the Festival of Torches (Candlemas) by illuminating the *Balsen*, i.e. the exits of caves, with torches in order to show the way back to the upper world to the souls retuning to the earth out of the "primeval state." (This

is the *Balfaribrauch*— from these *Balfen* the *Palfau* in Steirmark have their name.) Gods and humans celebrate *Fasnacht* [fasting-night = Lent] and *Fasing* [= *Fasching* = *Mardi Gras*], when the ship of Nehalenia departs to spread its fructifying blessings.

3. *Lenzmond*, March, Aries ♈: Saga in Söcquabeckr [Sökkvabekkr] (Plunge-brook). Snow and ice thaw and the feminine element, water, is liberated by the solar fire, the masculine element. Therefore All-Father's month-name, Nikar, also means "sun of the water nymphs' [*Nixensonne*]. The mild storms of spring rush over the murmuring waters — the speech of the waves is heard whispering. Wuotan, "reawakened," leads his army of souls without bodies to Lady Saga — who is none other than Freya — to unite the disembodied souls with the soulless bodies, which she brings out of her Sun-fortress, in order to render the effect of death harmless. Solar fire and earthly water hold a conversation. Wuotan and Saga "drink daily the drink of memory from golden horns."[10] The first swallow returns (Annunciation of Mary), the first violet blooms (violet festival), people celebrate the festival of spring, the festival of the Resurrection.

4. *Ostermond*, April, Taurus ♉: Wuotan in Glastheim [radiant-world]. The Sun has once more gained a complete victory (Hnikudr) on the day of the spring equinox, and now Wuotan appears as a groom just as he was active as a suitor in the previous month. His bride is the Earth-Goddess who also has as many names and aspects corresponding to them, as does the Sun-god himself. As Freya appeared as Lady Saga in the previous month, she is now Ostara, and the marriage of the divine pair takes place with the full Moon after the equinox. This is then a "high time" in heaven (Glastheim) and from this our concept of marriage [*Hochzeit*: literally "high-time"] has its origin. "High time" means the time of the Sun, and therefore our German concept *Hochzeit* knows nothing of a corresponding "low time."

5. *Mai*, May, Gemini ♊: Skadi (*Schade* [= harm, scathe]) in Thrimsheim. The second divine marriage follows soon after the first, but this one is not a *Hochzeit*, but rather only a marriage, as only the Sun can have a "high time," or zenith. After the Sun, the *Urfyr*, is wed to the Earth, the water now again weds the Earth, and these then form two related pairs. One pair is Donar [Thor] (weather-god) with Sabia (Earth-goddess) and the other, that comes into consideration here, is the giant-daughter, Skadi [scather] (once more the Earth) with the Rain-god, Niord. The first storm rains down in the mountains of Thrimsheim; Doner [Thor] killed the giant Thiassi and the Ases burned him in Asgard. His daughter requests legal compensation for the death of her father and is given permission to choose a groom from among the circle of the Ases, with the condition that she may only see the "left foot[11] of the various gods. She then goes for the one that looks most powerful to her and cries out: "Baldur is without blemish!" But she was mistaken; she had matched herself with the Rain-god not the Sun-god. The gods celebrate this wedding in Asgard and humans attend the Festival of Pentecost. There is yet a third wedding of the Earth-goddess with the Storm-god, Wuotan (air), that could be mentioned, but only one name recalls this wedding, which otherwise appears to have been totally

forgotten, the name is *Windesbraut* [wind-bride]. This is the Earth which appears to be seduced into a cloud of dust by the storm. Fire, water and air strive after the Earth to impregnate her. This is the meaning of this complex institution of divine marriage, many more of which could be named, and therefore in this month All-Father is called Fjöllnir, the Manifold.

6. *Brachet*, June, Cancer ♋: Baldur in Breidablik (Broad-view). The Sun is at its full power, ascended to its highest height [*Hochzeit*, zenith ~ marriage], when Hodur's deadly shot hits Baldur. Gods and humans are seized by wild terror and fearful anxiety, for Oski, the Ase who has every ability, has been killed off. The Ases prepare a funeral pyre for the Fallen Baldur and his things along with his dead wife, Nana. Humans attend the Midsummer festival (summer solstice).

7. *Heuet*, July, Leo ♌: Heimdal (Heimdoldt) in Himingbiörg [heaven's fortress]. Heimdoldt, the sentinel of the gods, stands on the highest battlement of his heavenly fortress and remains on the lookout as to whether the sons of Muspell are approaching, in which case the air will be glowing, or whether the dark rime- and frost-giants are trying to approach, in which case the white Sword-god will be vacillating and sinking and Darkness will begin its struggle with the primal light [*Urlicht*] all over again. Heimdoldt blows into his horn and all the high gods gather around him and anxiously hear as to whether the twofold danger is calling them to the final battle. The festival of the summer solstice goes on, fire flickers from every hilltop to frighten away the forces of darkness, if they should break out against the forces of light. *Omi, omen, amen!*

8. *Aust*, August, Virgo ♍: Freya in Volkwang. The danger has now been partially allayed. But the generative power of nature is growing tired, of course, and the ripening fruit is pressing on toward being harvested. Like Baldur, many a man has fallen in battle and so too have many fruits ripened on the tree of humanity only to sink once more into the grave. Souls are separated from bodies in battle [*Wal*] and All-Father and Freya each take their half. The former takes the souls who lost their bodies, and the latter takes care of the bodies having lost their souls, which she takes to Volkwang in the meadow of the dead. (Fridhof)(12), while Wuotan calls the liberated souls to Walhalla. However, the souls which have not yet attained to the level of free spirits go to Donar in Thrutheim, to Hel in Helheim, or to even darker places, each according to the soul's level of development. The bodies being held in Volkwang await their new reception of souls or spirits just as those souls contained in Walhalla and the other soul-worlds await their re-incarnation, each according to the measure of the powers which have prepared them and the gifts which have enriched them. The powers absorbed there thus strengthen them in this way (more on this later). All-Father-Biflindi, just as Freya-Fria feel their powers waning, and by providing rich harvests they provide for the 'primeval state," in order thereby to gather new forces for the coming battles. Wuotan,(13) who up until now has been the exhaling Giver,(14) now becomes the Taker when he inhales— therefore he is at this time the Shifty-One. The gods, like humans, are mindful of the cares of winter and begin, each for him or herself, to make harvest.

9. *Scheiding*, September, Libra ♎: Forsetti in Glitnir. The struggles and troubles continue on, the high gods hold council and take their places on their seats of judgment. Forsetti (the chief of the divine judges, son of Baldur) decides and discovers justice; he is actually All-Father himself as Vitnir, the generator of law. (Freya as ♍ holds the ♎.) Spirit and body, day and night, maintain their balance, gods and men deem that every sort of strife is put to rights and they come together for a common purpose; high-holy legal assemblies [things] are called, great popular assemblies are held, the fruits redden on the trees, the ears of corn become golden, the great general festival of the harvest draws near for gods and men alike.

10. *Gilbhart*, October, Scorpio ♏: Niord in Noatun (boat-home). Niord rules in the realm of ships which have returned to harbor. The ship is also symbolically the cradle and the coffin— and therefore the earth itself, upon which gods and men sail through cosmic space. Just as the ship of Nehalenia went out in Hornung to pour out blessings, it now comes home loaded down with the products of harvest. But the decisions have not proven themselves to be enduring; the light is increasingly at a disadvantage with regard to the darkness, All-Father-Svidrir allows that which has been generated to fade and he himself approaches a descent into *Ur*.

11. Laubris, November, Sagittarius ♐: Widar in Landwidi (woodland, rule-land [*Waltland*]). All-Father-Svidur sinks back into *Ur*. Wuotan-Hangatyr "consecrates himself to himself," as a self-sacrifice by hanging in the branches of Yggdrasil. From his semen, which falls down when he dies, the *Alraun* [mandrake root] grows up from the earth under the hanged-one. This is the re-born Wuotan under the name Widar "again" [*Wieder*]). Wiedar is therefore Svidur, who has returned, but only as his ancestor, and therefore only his formal appearance, his double [*Doppelgänger*]. Therefore he is also known as the silent Ase; but also the strongest, for he at once sets out and kills the murderer of Baldur, Hödur (Hader), whom he commends to the burning fortress (cremation) in the following month. When, according to other myths, Widar is seen as the son of Rind — the frozen earth in winter — this is just another image of the same process. But Widar also means the winter-sun, which is silent — i.e. without power — but in spite of this when he is called the strong, even the strongest, Ase after Donar, this refers to his reserve of power collected in the harvest which he takes down into *Ur* in order to transform this reserve there into even more power for his next return as the youthful solar god. He is the archer who refuses to shoot (Hubertus) because the arrows of the Sun are powerless at this time. For this reason too, the *tyr*-rune ᛏ struck through ♐ is the symbol of this zodiacal sign. The gods have descended into *Ur*, the migratory birds have left us, nature has grown quiet and humans celebrate the great festival of the dead (All Souls).

12. *Wihimanoth*, Yule-month, December ♑: Uller in Ydalir. The last month in the ring of the year, which contains the shortest day of the year as well as the longest night — the great Mother Night — in which the new Sun, the new time, is born. The role which Forsetti played in the inner life of man, as that of the one who decides in conflicts between

gods and giants, the spiritual and the material— is now taken on by Uller in the outer world as the one who decides on who is to win battles. Forsetti puts things to right through decisions and reconciliations, Uller though duels, for in his month the duel between the hostile brothers Wali and Hödur (Hader) takes place, the duel between light and darkness, between summer and winter. "Therefore it is good to call on him in all duels."[15] The gods prepare the funeral pyre for Hödur (Harder) and celebrate the birth of the young god of the Sun, while humans celebrate the holy-night and the fires of Yule.

Now it is remarkable that one month-god, namely Wali — the "Thirteenth"! — appears in Hornung in the solar-house Walaskialf, as well as in Laubris in the solar fortress Landwidi, without being at home in either fortress. This is actually the Thirteenth, the Dead-one. Wali is, as his name indicates, the dead. Walaskialf certainly belongs to Wuotan as Wal-Father, for it is Walhalla itself and Landwidi is Widar's property, but it is often confused with that of Wali. Widar is not the killer of Hödur, but rather it is Wali, who only "gets off his horse's back in Widar's forested homeland," for his solar house, the thirteenth, was lost to him when the twelve solar months displaced the thirteen lunar months. But Wali will rise up again and he even survives the twilight of the gods [Göttrdämmerung] along with Widar. Thus he was compelled, even if temporarily, as if he was being sheltered, to be placed in "Widar's forested homeland" in Landwidi.

But the Twelve-Gods also — like the Seven-Gods — can be brought back to the "high holy three," that is to the "three holy times" and the "three great recurring Things," the ancient German high times for holding court.

The foremost of the three high-holy times corresponds to the well-known "high holy Three"— arising, becoming, passing away to a new arising (or transformation) and comprised Holy-night [Yule], Easter, and the great festival of the dead. The other holy Three were above all incorporated as recurrent Things, as times for holding court and fell in Hornung, May and on St. Michael's Day as the most important Thing of the year, the *Mihilathing* [September 29].

As it is not the task of this work to provide a Aryo-Germanic mythology, but rather to explain the Aryo-Germanic *Wihinei* ["religion"] in the main aspects of its secret doctrine as Armanism, as well as in its use as a folk-religion or Wuotanism (and the latter as comprehensively as possible), this brief presentation of the mythology should suffice since it provides the key for anyone to be able to understand the larger mythological works and analyze them according to *Wihinei*. But before we go any further toward the goals lying before us, the basis should be laid out according to which every mythological name, every mythological object, every mythological event and every mythological prediction (prophesy) can be evaluated and determined immediately in its Armanic or Wuotanic meaning. Furthermore this is equally transferable to the exact sciences— for *Wihinei* and knowledge [*Wissen*] are one! **Wihinei has its strength in that it does not desire or require blind faith, but rather only advances empirical principles and does not merely allow, but rather makes into a duty** that individuals should gather experience and knowledge and only believe that which they know. This certain, indubitable knowledge should, however, also be made manifest in the way they conduct their lives. The caretakers and preservers of *Wihinei*, the *Armanen* or *Semanen* (the word "priest" is too restrictive) knew very well, however, that the great mass of the people would not be up to such a tremendous task and so they clothed their teachings in stories and names which immediately offer the thinker the correct interpretation— if only he knows and comprehends the key, i.e. the method of analysis. He thus also has the possibility of investigating further. How the characteristic words and names — so-called code-words [*Kennworte*] — are to be analyzed, has already been shown in many examples. (There is more about this in Guido-von-List-Bücherei Nr. 6: *Die Ursprache der Ario-Germanen.*) Furthermore, it has been repeatedly emphasized that all events are divided up according to the Three-Stages: arising, becoming, transformation (passing away to a new arising), a tripartition which, however, is expanded under certain conditions into heptads, enneads (more about these later), twelvefold models, and other numeric arrangements. Also mention has been made of the masculine essence consisting of light, fire, warmth, spirit— as well as the feminine essence comprising darkness, water, cold, matter, etc. This duality originated from an androgynous or double-sexed (not hybrid or hermaphroditic) unity. Equally, however, that duality was thought of in all cases which would be characteristic of the "bifidic-biune dyad" [*beideinig-zwiespältige Zweieinheit*], for example the *Ur*-element which arose through the condensation of spirit into *Ur*-matter and which is therefore indivisibly bound to the spirit, one with it but nevertheless forming a dyad (spirit-body or spirit-matter). From this latter principle it clearly and irrefutably follows that both spirit and matter are eternal, but that spirit is the immutable essence while matter, which merely signifies the visible form of spirit, is finite and mutable and upon dissolution resolves itself into spirit again and ceases to be the visible form of the spirit. But as dissolved matter, i.e. as spirit itself, it is eternal— eternal without beginning and without end.

Thus spirit, before its condensation to *Ur*-matter, is the uncaused cause, the unnamed and unrevealed God. When this unnamed and unrevealed God, by his will to reveal himself, inhaled and condensed himself, thereby calling matter into existence, he emerged from his concealment, revealed himself— and this event is called the First Logos. That was the beginning of time (one thing after the other) and space (one thing next to the other), which, since apparent forms are temporal, i.e. not eternal, for each has a beginning and an end, thus occurred the first effect of the causeless cause. In this first revealed form, as the First Logos, the inconceivable and ineffable *Great Spirit* appears under the name Surtur, i.e. *s'ur-t'ur*: From *Ur* to *Ur*, or All-Father (*Allfatur*, i.e. *Al* = all; *fat* = generate; *ur* = "the primeval"— the All-generator out of the primeval). But, of course, he is still *Ur* itself, primeval matter [*Urstoff*], primeval material that evolved itself in constant arising, becoming and transformation into the entire cosmos as a "biune-bifurcated biunity." As *Ginnungagap* he is himself the one who created his own space; as "Wuotan, Donar, Loki" (= was-is-becomes) he is self-created time; as

"All-Father, Wuotan, Donar, Loki and Gerda" he is the five elements—
i.e. aether, fire, air, water and earth; as Urda, Werdandi and Skuld he is
the causeless cause, the cause of all causes which have effects, of all
events created by and through him; as Wuotan and Frigga he is the
unified androgynous being which is divided into fire-water, warmth-cold,
light-darkness, day-night, spirit-matter, soul-body, etc., in order to be
unified, and unified in order to be divided.

This becomes even clearer in the diagram on page 21.

If the schematic of creation is clearly characterized here through the
three levels of arising, becoming, transformation (passing away toward a
new arising), the first basic rule to be derived from this has to be called
the law of *homogeneity* (*analogy*). Everything in living nature takes place
according to this law, and one only has to remember the pattern "bud-
bloom-fruit" to recognize this principle of homogeneity.

In connection with this tripartition a certain dark interval is at once
obvious which seemingly interrupts the chain of events between the
passing away while the stage between new arising and passing away is
characterized as *becoming*. This becomes clearer when another
terminology is used, i.e. being born, living, and dying. It is self-evident
that life is the counter-pole of death, for just as life stands between birth
and death, death lies between dying and being born, and in this way
completes the circle.(16) And thus we have arrived at a principal form of
Armanic knowledge in which *the law of homogeneity* is primarily
asserted. It has already been shown and demonstrated in connection with
the biune-bifidic biunity of spirit and matter that spirit and body are
indivisible, but not soul and body, which are separate entities. Here the
soul is provisionally called the "self" [*Ichheit*] (individuality, the body on
the other hand may be characterized as the essence [*Wesenheit*]
(personality).

Since the soul emerges from the *Ur* more or less in a complete state and returns to the *Ur* after the death of the body in order to be reborn, as has been said above it is as eternal as spirit, and so the "ego" (individuality) must be immortal. As spirit it is eternal. But as a soul it is born in the moment of the revelation of the First Logos, when spirit is poured in a rayified way into matter, as a part of the great demiurge. Every *soul* is just such a ray, which is only extinguished — but does not cease — when the revealed God dissolves matter by means of his exhalation and returns to a state of pure spirit. Thereupon all projected rays return to the *Ur*-spirit — Surtur — and again become one with it. The soul is at the same time also a spiritual body and disembodies itself only with the cessation of the spiritual body of the divinity, of the demiurge, i.e. at the moment of the dissolution of matter, when All-Father — the World-Spirit — once more becomes Surtur through exhalation just as it had incarnated itself at the moment when Surtur condensed spirit into *Ur*-matter by means of inhalation and he projected it as a ray from within himself into the material world.

The next inference now becomes self-evident. Every soul is a part of the divinity itself; every soul was in God before the emergence of the First Logos. But since before the First Logos there was neither space (one thing next to another) nor time (one thing after another), there could therefore only be the One, and so every soul in this circumstance was itself God, and also remains in the purely spiritual sense in its present condition nothing more and nothing less than God itself. Only in its spiritually embodied condition — considered without a terrestrial body — is it an "ego" (individuality) as something different from other souls— or egos (individualities).

It has already been said that every atom has a soul, but that the life, the spirit, slumbering in a latent manner from the beginning only gradually awakens in it. The more advanced atomic souls which awakened earlier than the others also acquired earlier than the others a greater power and thereby gained the force to subjugate the atoms that are only ensouled with a latent spirit. Thus by and by the seven elements arose from *Ur*-matter (*Ginnungagap*), and from these elements the great heavenly bodies were formed, including the earth. The spirit or soul of the Earth is not All-Father, the World-Spirit, but rather All-Father-Wuotan, the Earth-Spirit and as such he is the Second Logos as relates to our Earth. Therefore it is only he, as humans came into existence, who could breathe the divine spirit (= *Odem*, therefore Odin = Wuotan) into them, for his two brothers, the Ases (those who bear the pillars of the earth)[18] were only able to create their bodies. However, if one follows the step-ladders upward from the unconscious souls of the elements, of minerals, to the more conscious ones of plants and to the even more developed ones of animals, one will easily recognize with the inner eye the ascent of the souls toward a higher evolution if one imagines that every soul — each maintaining a consistent individuality or ego — has passed though its process of development from below upward through the elements and minerals, through the vegetable and animal worlds up to that stage of evolution which it possesses today and that it will perfect itself in constant ongoing evolution up to its highest ability to evolve, the pinnacle of which has to be the re-winning of perfect divinity which was formerly lost due to the process of being solidified into matter. But between animal and human there exists a chasm that cannot be bridged and over which animals cannot pass, for humans did not evolve out of the animal world, but rather it is often the other way around as unfortunately many species of animals are descended from humans by means of unnatural hybridizations.(19)

Armanism has, as we have shown above, already long since recognized and explained this chasm between the animal kingdom and the world of humanity on this Earth, which modern science has not yet been successful in filling in or bridging. Nor will it ever be successful in this as long as it persists in its purely materialistic theories of today. Wuotanism knows Mannus as the progenitor of humanity; Armanism, however, sees in this name a code-word, which is clear enough: man = "man" and "Moon," and us = "out of" [aus], i.e. "The man from the Moon," or the lunar ancestors.

A high secret of the "high secret Acht" is this anthropogenesis in that it reveals that the Moon is older than the Earth and is its father, but that the Moon is today in a transformational state— of passing away to a new arising. The Moon shrank up, became smaller and weaker, and gave over its living spirits to the earth which now compels it — as its captive — to follow the Earth as a satellite. Since, as the older and more evolved of the two, the Moon had a population spiritually far superior to that of the Earth, this population was transplanted to Earth in the form of humanity, which explains the spiritual ascendancy of terrestrial humanity descended from lunar ancestors, as compared to those who spiritually belong to the Earth and who had by and by evolved as the highest living beings of the animal kingdom. The lunar ancestors also brought with them the formation of the human body, a property which they bequeathed to the Earth, and for this reason the human body manifests a special characteristic form which distinguishes it as something which arose suddenly and not as something that emerged in the course of evolution from an animal body. Therefore the missing link between the animal kingdom and the plane of humanity is nowhere to be found, for it never existed. However, there have been certain reversions to type evolving humans back to the level of animals— the ape-men (see the investigations of Dr. J. Lanz von Liebenfels). The animal kingdom of the earth will also be lifted to the level of humanity in the coming cycles of the earth in the ages of the Sixth and Seventh Root Races, and at the end of the seventh cycle they too will reach the level of divinity for themselves.

With the emergence of humanity on our earth, with the inception of the age of the Third Logos, the reverberation of divinity in humanity had arrived, and thus a new evolutionary period began for the Earth itself.

We have already acknowledged that the soul is in and of itself a ray of divinity projected by the divinity at that moment when it poured itself out into matter. From this point on, which is at the same time the beginning of time itself, every soul is an ego-consciousness [Ichheit] in its own right, an ego or individuality which it constantly remains until at the end of time it returns to God, and since the end of time also heralds the end of space, the soul becomes God. As such every soul with an ego or individuality, along with every atom, has its general mission [Sendung] which exists within it, and at the end of time and space they return to the divinity (Surtur, the Holy Spirit) in order to become one with it. In addition to its general mission it also has a special mission which the ego most especially must accomplish and for the purpose of this accomplishment it must go its special way, which forms an uncommon and complex weave-work along with the special pathways of numerous other souls. For purposes of accomplishing this special mission upon each rebirth the soul assumes a new and different essence (personality), an essence which is an expression of the given body (as a human this would be the human body), which the soul builds up in conjunction with the task that must be fulfilled in the subsequent human life. The soul, especially that of a human being, is therefore comparable to an actor who sometimes wears the mask of a king, then that of a beggar, or a fool, or a criminal, or a saint, or a martyr. These masks must present his personalities or essences, while he — as an **ego** — always remains the same individuality, just as the same soul, whose body is only a transitory mask for this or that role, it has to perform in the great play of becoming.

The primary mission of all souls, and therefore of all individuals, is that of fulfilling and realizing the will of God, which is logically their own will as well. The will of God as the world-spirit (First Logos) was to break through latent stasis, to become active through creating, and to discover himself within himself as he fully experiences every joy — but every form of suffering as well — in order to find stasis once more in the *Ur* having been saturated by both joy and suffering, and to live on there after the cessation of time and space within itw own memory. Therefore even the universe did not come into existence in a finished state, so there is continuous new-arising, becoming, metamorphosis, passing away and renewed arising in order to create things anew continuously, and therefore a great complexity resides within the revealed divinity, or cosmos, and so nothing repeats itself in nature, for change is the only constant in becoming. Therefore man is called upon to help construct the works of God, which are also his own, and therefore he is moved to action by dark urges and instincts, for he desires — working unconsciously in the will of God — to create new things continually, as man desires change. He loves that which is ancient — memory! — but he doesn't want to relive it over and over again, but rather he wants to create something new built upon the old, in order to enjoy the new. This is because the ancient, that which has already been lived out, has already been used up by him in his earlier lives and now he wants to create, experience and enjoy, something new once again. But by doing this he often falls into numerous errors. Sometimes he forgets the spiritual side of things and thus sinks down into a materialistic existence(20) so that he has to suffer through many rebirths in order to rediscover his lost sense of inwardness [Innerlichkeit]. Another time he might neglect the material world too much, become a deluded dreamer, lose the ground beneath his feet and die of starvation. In either case he will have forgotten that he should think, feel and act in a spiritual-corporeal [geist-körperlich] way, and that as long as he walks upon the earth in a body of flesh and blood he is called to serve both spiritual and material affairs in a balanced manner. Such mistakes in thought, feeling, action and omission of these things do not, however, remain without consequences, for all thought, feeling, action and omission of such things constitute causes which lead to effects, which in turn become causes of further effects. Such a series of cause and effect is known as a chain of causality, each of which is to be traced back to the uncreated cause, the First Logos— *Urda*.(21) This is the Garmic Law we have delineated as "Urda-Werdandi and Should" in the Nornic Triad.

Every self [*Ichheit*], especially every human self, creates its own "Garmic chain" (chain of causality), which it cannot escape. But this self is in a position to guide its *Garma* (destiny) toward its best goals as it always — like Freya and Forsetti — maintains a balance ♎ between the spiritual and physical, never losing sight of the eternal — through its conscience — constantly holding its thoughts and feelings, action and inaction, in balance.

But the individual ego [*Ich*], as an individuality, is caught up in Garmic chains other than its own; for no self [*Ichheit*] stands alone, but rather it is only part of a group. Groups join together to form larger circles and so forth until they encompass everything generally. The next set of groups to which the individual ego is subordinated is that of the family, then the tribe, then the community [*Gemeinde*], the people [*Volk*], the state, the race, humanity, the earth, the solar system, the next higher systems of the central sun, and so forth — who can say to what levels!? — until one reaches the All-Father himself. If Wuotanism only takes us to the Sun ☉, beyond which it posits the Divine Sun (Psychelia) ☉, and indicates no further connecting links, it is just keeping to that which is perceptible. But Armanism knows that there are no limits, neither in magnitude upwards, nor in smallness downward, and that only an infinitesimally small part of this chain running from the greatest things to the smallest can ever become conscious through the senses. Every smallest atom is confined to the circle of a larger one into which it is incorporated, this is again so contained in a circle that is greater still, etc., until it becomes a corpuscle in the human body, and remains confined there. The individual person again appears incorporated within his family, etc., all the way up to the Earth-spirit, and this in turn is subordinated to the Solar spirit, and this in turn is subordinated to a series of ever-increasing circles up to the All-Father, the great universal spirit [*Universalgeist*], all of which have their Garma, and thus influence the Garma of the selves [*Ichheiten*] incorporated within their circles. So the individual self has a part in the Garma of its family, its tribe, its community, its people [*Volk*], state, etc., right up to the Garma of the All-Father himself, for the entire All is just that — the Great One — that which is revealed in the First Logos itself.

If the self in question is therefore born into, for example, a royal family, then the Garma of this family will influence his individual Garma, just as his Garma will in return influence that of the family. If that royal family perhaps even loses its position of power through the fault of this individual and descends during the course of ages to an insignificant level, then the Garma of that self, incorporated within that family, will be influenced over time in such a way that the selves [*Ichheiten*] born at the time of this nadir will also have their sphere of power reduced. Since, however, each self is, as a rule, reborn into its own family,(22) and since it cannot escape from the circle in which it is incorporated, it is true that every self was — as an essence (personality) — its own ancestor just as it will be its own descendent. In this way it realizes its own Garma, in the good or bad sense, in the course of subsequent rebirths. ('The sins of the fathers avenge themselves on their descendants to the seventh generation." [Paraphrased from Genesis 34.7]) But their virtues are also credited to an equal degree, for Freya and Forsetti hold the scales ♎. Therefore this Garma is neither vengeance nor punishment, neither benefit nor reward, but rather simply the effect of one of several causes, and thus it is possible for the individual self, once it finally has recognized the laws of Garma, to effect causes which bring about favorable effects, i.e. to be able to construct a fortunate Garma, not only for the present life but for future rebirths as well, and not only for one's self but for one's family, tribe, community, state,(23) etc. The "Nornic web," as Wuotanism calls these Garmic chains, form the basis of the "Nornic fabric for the raiment of the ages," as Wuotanism characterizes the whole of the Garmic chains all linked up. From this it is self-evident that there exists no meaningless fate, that no thought is lost, but rather every thought, every word, every action and every omission of any kind has its particular influence upon the All and its own Garma, whose significance in this world of illusion and error can not be completely estimated. All of this would cast us into doubt if we did not already know that Garma has a conscious direction toward the Good, and that its dark, apparently confusing and erroneous, paths are in fact not erroneous paths at all, but rather — without exception — they all lead "through the night toward the light." This divine guidance — aware and certain of its own aims — is entirely conscious within every self in its dark impulse, and this consciousness is called the "conscience," or the "inner voice." Every self which follows this inner voice will acquire good Garma; everyone who works against it, however, generates bad Garma, even if other effects seem to be manifested at first. The old folk saying and admonition: "the millstones of God grind slowly, but exceedingly fine" brings the truth of this to mind, as all genuine old sayings always contain a grain of esoteric truth. This inner voice, the *conscience*; which is actually the unconscious perceptive feeling for what is right, is in fact the unbreakable thread that connects the individual self [*Ichheit*] with the divinity and enables the self to guide its manifestations (personalities) rightly through the world of humanity, and gradually to conduct them in a sure way back to God throughout many rebirths.

Now since every self possesses this inner voice, more or less developed in a way corresponding to the level of its own development, it is also true that every self may seek a direct connection through this voice with the Godhead itself, which is therefore not outside of the heart, not "up there beyond the vault of stars," but rather within the self, in its own heart, and this awareness is called "the inwardness of God" [*Gottinnerlichkeit*]. Those fortunate ones who know how to find God within themselves no longer need a intercessor, or priest, they have arrived at a stage of "self-priesthood," their heart is the tabernacle in which they carry God contained within themselves. Their whole being [*Ich*] is the sanctuary [*Halgadom*] of the Godhead itself, and their whole lives are self-sacrifices which they dedicate to the God within and thereby also dedicate themselves directly to the All-Father himself. Therefore our ancient ancestors called this "inwardness of God," and the self-evolving self-sanctification [*Selbstweihe*] developing out of it, by its correct name: *Wihinei*, i.e. "the inward sanctification," while it is otherwise called by its Latin name: *religion*. But religion means "reconnection (with God)," which indicates a condition in which the original "inwardness of God" is obscured. This inwardness is already seen as something which has been lost, while the concept *Wihinei* presupposes the full possession of the inwardness of God and thus indicates a higher ethical concept.

The concept of self [*Ichheit*] (individuality) always remains the same from the beginning of the First Logos forward to the dissolution of the spirit and the cessation of time and space. This is in contrast to the concept of the essence [*Wesenheit*] (personality), which is temporarily bounded by life and death— and thus the concept of self obviously indicates the complete exclusion of a condition of destruction and amends the concept of death accordingly, such that "death" is merely life in the primeval state [*Urständ*] and only means a cessation of the essence or substance [*Wesenheit*]. Now since, however, every self, as soon as it is reborn, creates a new substance (personality) as a phenomenological form according to its lower or higher Garmic development; it has actually prepared for itself the conditions for its new life in a human body on the basis of its own thought, feeling, speech, action and inaction in previous lives in human bodies. So the self continues the fulfillment of its special position according to the degree of its development in these newly begun human lives, i.e. it begins this activity at the level where it was interrupted in its last life.

In order to make this more understandable by means of an example, in accordance with the *law of homogeneity* let's take a painter. He is conceiving of a plan for a picture. He lies down to sleep at night, after he has undressed (died), that night he dreams of his planned work (preparation in the primeval state) and rises early in the morning (is reborn) and gets right to work. He draws the initial sketch on the canvas, primes it, etc. The evening comes and he once more goes to bed after he has laid aside his raiment (substance, personality) and goes to sleep (dies) once again. Once more he awakens (is reborn) in order to continue his work where he had left off the day before. Thus many days (lives in human bodies) pass, and just as many nights (primeval states), but the work gradually continues to move toward its completion. Many more days and nights pass, but finally his work — let's say on the seventieth day — is finished and he receives a good price for it. Is being born and dying really so different from getting up in the morning and going to sleep at night? We see in the history of inventions how many centuries it it took before the discovery of the power of steam could be turned into steam-machines, locomotives and steamships. There were enormous intervals, spanning centuries, between the individual experiments and the time when completed inventions could come into general use. Is this any

29

different from the example of the painter and his picture? How many rebirths did, for example, the self of Vasco de Garay, who traveled on the Danube for the first time by means of a steamboat in 1543, have to go through before it once more traveled by steamer on the Seine as Robert Fulton on the 9th of February 1803? What courses of development did this self have to undertake in the past and what lies ahead of it still? For, that there exists a connection through reincarnation between Garay and Fulton cannot be rejected out of hand.

If, though recognition of the necessity of rebirth, certainty has now been gained(24) concerning the continuation of life in death beyond the grave, then the no-less understandable certainty follows that without acceptance of rebirth or reincarnation there could be no development in the story of mankind, as this would otherwise always stall out in the stages of initial advances, if there was no rebirth, and every newly created self would have to start over from the beginning. It would be like a tangled mess of almost countless individual beginnings instead of an organically constituted evolution with conscious aims and certainties consisting of a harmonious cooperation of numerous selves who form the warp and woof of the *Nornic fabric* on the loom of the raiment of the ages in order to make the *Nornic weave-work* possible. As with every weave-work sometimes the thread (self) runs on top, visible (as the essence in a human body) then once more underneath (in the primeval state, in death) and invisible, only to reemerge visibly once more and thus contribute its part to the pattern of the whole. If one were to pull just one thread out of a tapestry— e.g. out of a Gobelin[25] — the whole work of art would be ruined, but yet again, how difficult it is to trace a single thread the whole way through when one looks at the entire work! It appears insignificant, yet it is precisely in this way that individual selves behave within the All— they seem to disappear in the All, and yet the All would no longer be the All if just one of them were to be lacking.

In the *Law of Garma* the highest form of justice belonging to the ruling — and this should be emphasized — the *consciously* ruling deity is both concealed and established. Every self [*Ichheit*] has to bear the same mission, the same path, the same measure of suffering and joy, which is doled out among all its many reincarnations. It is therefore more than shortsighted to compare in a correlative manner the life-conditions of one's contemporaries and from this comparison draw any conclusions from the results. In every individual substantive life of those now living only *one* phase of rebirth is visible, and we are in no way able to get even the smallest overview of the whole chain of rebirths. Such a judgment would be as nonsensical as if one were to cut out a pea-sized piece from each painting in a large collection of thousands of paintings and thoroughly mix up all the little pieces and then venture to make a judgment on the value of the art of painting from the resulting montage. None of us is in a position to evaluate correctly the self [*Ichheit*] of another by observing its present life, no matter how well-known it is to us. This is because at best we can only know a large part — and not even the entirety — of its mask, of its outer substance, but nothing of its inner self which remains its own innermost property and the secret of each individual self. We can therefore hardly recognize the traits emerging from this self's Garmic developmental process, but the hidden threads of the earlier and incidental Garmic reflections can not be recognized at all. Indeed the least of us will have their self-knowledge so submerged that they will only know their own Garma. The comforts life offers them they accept as a given, the discomforts, which they rightly know in most cases to be their own fault, are rejected with moans and laments as undeserved accidents and they blame the deity for being unjust. Indeed undeserved accidents actually do occur often enough in this life, just as completely unearned strokes of luck do, but these are actually rooted in the Garma from earlier lives in human bodies, as a result of actions whose roots only very rarely become conscious, which, however, always follow Garmic laws and therefore accord with the perfect justice of the consciously ruling deity. Furthermore, it should be considered that our ancient ancestors, especially those belonging to the early stages of humanity, lived in less than enviable conditions that are hardly comparable to our lives today, and that we ourselves are in large measure establishing, or at least preparing the way for, the improvement of the living conditions of our descendants, without ourselves benefiting from this improvement. This would constitute a limitation of the pleasures of life for the ancestors in relation to the dependents if it were not the case that the ancestors were their own descendants **in that without exception all selves live through all ages with only brief interruptions which they spend in the primeval state.** The length of time for the stay of the self in the primeval state [*Urständ*] after the death of the substance (personality) should, according to the law of homogeneity, last about as long as the length of life in the human body, for day and night are almost in balance, although on average the day exceeds the length of night. But now the question of what the self does in the primeval state, and what it can expect there, must be answered. To be able to answer this question we must go back in more detail to the foundational heptads and the nine abodes of the gods.

As to how the All (everything) evolved from the One and nevertheless remains One, i.e. the All-one (whence the misunderstood and misused saying "Everything is One"), and subsequently formed the polyvalent-polyunified poly-unity(26) and in a further intensification the all-valent–all-unified all-unity,(27) has already been alluded to in these discussions, but they should be even more soundly explained.

The series of stages for this is as follows: The monad: i.e. Surtur the Great Spirit. Holy Spirit.

[The dyads.] The "bifurcated bi-unified Bi-unity": The revealed god, All-Father, the World-Spirit ☉, the First Logos: Ginnunga-gap, the *Ur*-element, Spirit-Body: androgyne, bi-sexual reproduction: light and darkness, warmth and coldness, day and night; sexual reproduction: man and woman.

The triads: "trifurcated triunified Tri-unity. The Three-Gods: Wuotan, Wili, We; Har, Jafnhar, Thridri; Wuotan, Donar, Loki; Freya, Frauwa, Frigga; Urda, Verdandi, Skuld. The "three-things": Yggdrasil with the three wells, three roots, three branches (3 x 3, see below concerning nine), arising, becoming, transition; past, present, future (time); height, width, depth (space); three holy times, etc.(28)

The tetrads: The first four known elements fire (Muspellsheim), water (Adhumbla), air (Niflheim), earth (Ymir). The four ages: the golden, the silver, the bronze and the iron. The four conditions of the self [*Ichheit*] as an essence: arising (birth), becoming (life in a human body), transition (death), preparation for a new arising (death, life in the primeval state). The four dwarves of the quarters of heaven: Austri, Sudri, Vestri, Nordri (east, south, west and north), and many other tetrads, such as: four brothers, four women, four heads, four horns (corners) of heaven, four harts, four streams of milk, four oxen, four bulls, four gates, etc.

The pentads: The holy *Fem* (five), the five known elements (fire, water, air, earth, ether or aether), the five recognized senses (for, in fact, there are seven),(29) the pentagram, the five brothers, the five maidens, the five men, the five nights, the five sons, the five winters, etc.

The hexads: The hexagram (six-star), the sixth day (*sextac*).

The heptads: the seven rays of light (rainbow), seven fires, seven tones, seven goddesses of love, the seven gods, Sibia, seven years, seven senses, seven months, seven weeks, seven days, seven nights, seven winters, seven worlds, seven rounds, seven races, seven heavens, seven underworlds, seven she-eagles [*Adlerininnen*], seven half-years, seven kings, seven maidens, seven electors, seven halls, seven sisters, seven brothers, seven sons, seven springs, seven mountains, seven oaks, seven planets, seven-stared constellation, to swear an oath before seven [*besiebenen*].

The octads: The high holy eight [*Acht*]-tribunal. Eight eyes, eight brothers, eight nobles, eight feet, eight knaves, eight salmons, eight men, eight nights, eight days, eight resting places [*Rasten*], eight rings, eight sisters, eight parts, eight winters, etc.

The enneads: The nine divine worlds, the nine mothers of Heimdall, the nine valkyries, the nine wave-maidens (nixes), the nine branches, nine main songs, nine magical songs, nine kettles, nine knaves, nine maidens, nine-man work, nine feet wide, nine moons, nine nights, nine days, nine months, nine resting places [*Rasten*], nine realms, nine giant-daughters, nine palaces, nine steps, nine sisters, nine daughters, nine worlds, nine winters, nine wolves, etc.

The decad is only known to the great secret tribunal [*Acht*] of Armanism and signifies the creator or divine provider (*Gibor-altar*). It is formed from the three-gods and the seven-gods (3 + 7 = 10), which together make One, the One. Its sign is | (the *Is*-rune) surrounded by the *al*-circle, i.e. the *om*-sign ⊕[30]) = 10 and X (X), the sign of multiplication or the *Gibor*-rune X. The word *zehn* [ten] is derived from *ze, se* = "sun" and *han* = "contained" and thus means "containing divinity." On the basis of this was founded a *Zehnschaft* (*cennomani*), which served to bond a community around a *Halgadom* [temple] and in later times the tithe [tenth-part] (solar hand, solar property; here the sun is obviously understood as the spiritual sun ☉, as God, as All-Father and not as the physical sun ⊙). The concept of the "hundred," often substituted for the word *Zehnschaft*, is not connected with the numeral one hundred, but rather it comes from *huon, huun* = foundation, congregation, from which *hun* and *han* = judge, town council, is derived. Merely as an aside, it may be mentioned that the number 100 was called *zehnzig* ["tenty"], while *hundrathio, hundert* [hundred] indicated the number 120, which was later called the "great hundred."

As is virtually self-evident from this brief summary of the first ten words for numerals, these did not originate from dry numerical values, but rather have their origin in the developmental representation of the great evolutionary process (cosmogony), and signify the evolutionary stages of this process with very precise concepts, which only later become numerical values. And this knowledge is also the basis of the secret science of of numerical symbolism. From this standpoint let us take a look at the interpretation of the words for numerals we have already introduced:

One [*ein*] *en, een, einn, ains, an* derived from *ei, ai* = sun, therefore also "oath," "aiter-nettle," "egg," etc. The sun is the symbol of the "spiritual sun as God," and as such it is the epitome of the *One*, and thus once more the egg, as the world-egg, is the symbol of creation. Thus the *One* was developed as a numerical value from the concept of the revealed One, from its symbol - the *one* visible sun. The written sign for this numerical value is the *Is*-rune: "|" which was already shown in our discussion of "10" to be our usual notation | even today, and which corresponds to the Roman numeral I (*is* = is, to stand, to be constant, iron, ice, but also the "I").

As we have already shown, the symbol of zero is likewise derived from the holy-sign of the circle, which symbolizes the unrevealed God, and also the other numerical symbols — falsely called "Arabic" — were developed from the circle combined with the sign of multiplication, the *gibor*-rune: X which resulted in this matrix: ⊗.(31) The series of these holy number-runes which appear in the following manner in a 13th century manuscript in the Royal Imperial Library in Vienna, the so-called Imperial Chronicle: *1 2 3 4 7 6 8 9 0* , whence the old linear formations can still rather closely be made out. That these numerical signs have been referred to as "Arabic-Indian numerals" in more recent times, proves that belief in Aryanism is finally beginning to break through. Certainly the same thing is true for Sanskrit, but it should not be thought that Sanskrit is the root, but rather is is but one of the older branches of the Aryan world-tree, which was derived from proto-Aryan, like our Germanic languages. Therefore, it shares a common origin and is of the same age as our Germanic languages in which Old Aryan still lives.

Two (2, II) masculine *twai, twegen, zwêne, zween*; feminine *twos, two, zwo*; neuter *twa, tu, zwei*, only in New High German did the neuter form assert itself over all other genders. Since the primeval words *ta, za*, and *sa* are equivalent in meaning, it becomes self-explanatory as to how in many other words there is a sound change form *t* to *z*. *Ta, za, tu*, etc. means "to make, do" and therefore the sense of "doing, making, creating, shaping" still underlies the number two in the secret language of the high secret tribunal [*Acht*]. The concept "two," before it ever indicated a number, was therefore one of *creativity* and of the creator in its bisexual (androgynous) manifestation and later was transferred to the godhead divided into a masculine and feminine side to be reunited sexually— the **bifidic-biune-duo-unity**, and from this conceptual model the numerical value was only later developed.

1. Muspellsheim (primal fire), the seat of Al-fadur Surt (All-Father as the World-Spirit).
2. Alfheim, the seat of the light-elves (*liosalfar* = *lio* = light; *sal* = holiness; *far* = solar-generation, i.e. salvation generated through light and the sun).
3. Asaheim, godheim, the seat of the Ases, gods.
4. Wanaheim, the realm of the Vanes (those who perceive).
5. Mannaheim, the human world.
6. Jötunheim, the giant world.
7. Svartalfheim, the realm of the dwarves or dark-elves.
8. Helheim, hell.
9. Niflheim, the mist world.

Refraining from getting into more details on the meanings of the words, there are other enneads to be considered: these include the nine mothers of Heimdall, who actually correspond to the nine abodes, or the nine valkyries and other groups of nine things. Likewise the world ash, Yggdrasil, with its three roots, three springs and three branches, is to be provisionally referred to as an example of the inaccessibly high symbol of the high-holy threefold Tri-unity. Now, if the New-One is the God-Man himself in an esoteric-mystical interpretation, and if the thrice-holy nine is the hallowed number of perfected man, then the number ten is the Godhead itself, as we already showed above. Much more about number symbolism here world lead us too far afield, nevertheless we should, when the opportunity arises, take the meanings of such symbolism into account in the context of the present work.

The question does, however, come up as to what exactly gives rise to the self (the **unembodied soul**) in the primeval condition [*Urständ*], and what it has to do there.

First of all it must be shown that the human being is more than merely the spirit-body duality and that it is actually a self-contained heptad [sevenfoldedness] and thus a spirit-soul = $\triangle$ = and body = $\square$, which is composed in the following manner: 1. The spirit [*Geist*], the divine breath (Wuotan); 2. the spiritual soul and 3. the human soul. This triad differentiates humans from animals, over the level of which humanity is able to lift and maintain itself because it possesses these three— even if despite the possession of these faculties they often go unused. Animals on the other hand only possess an animal soul, which only will be able to be elevated to the level of human souls in future evolutionary cycles after the demise of the current Fifth Root Race. That upper, spiritual-psychic $\triangle$ of humanity, or the human self [*Ichheit*] is contrasted with the lower physical corporeal $\square$, which consists of: 1. the instinctual body, and the drive to good or evil action, 2. life, 3. the ethereal (astral) body and 4. the physical body.

These seven parts are closely connected to, but not inseparable from, one another, and are actually layered one over the other like the structure of an onion. The physical body provides the outer form of appearance, the substance of every self, but the other more subtle bodies cross the boundaries of the physical body and only become visible under special circumstances, and thus they sometimes become visible as the aura. Upon death the self casts off the physical body, which it leaves with the ethereal body, but it still possesses life, the instinctive body and all psychic characteristics. Yet even during the time when the self possesses a physical body it sometimes separates itself from that body. This usually occurs unconsciously during sleep when it hovers above the sleeping body like a light mist. Such separation can also occur due to darker causes (psychic doubles [*Doppelgänger*]) in somnambulistic states, etc. Sometimes , however, this can also also be caused by means of conscious willed effort. But the self does not yet slough off the substance (personality) along with the physical body, whether consciously or unconsciously, in life or upon death. The life-force slowly continues along its further transformations through the four upper or lower divine abodes. What the self immediately loses upon death, however, is the physical body and with it only the outer form of the substance (personality).

The folk belief of Wuotanism appoints to every self two protective spirits— *fylgjur*, following spirits — which urge the self to choose the right- or left-hand path, while the conscience— either the guardian of the gods, Heimdall, or the judge of the gods, Forsetti — passes judgment. These are the △: the spirit and the spiritual and human soul. The spirit holds the ♎ (scales) and the proper path is chosen according to whether the spiritual or human soul tips the scale.

In the upper realm as regards the nine abodes of the gods we have Mannaheim, the homeland of men or the world of humans, standing as the fifth in the series, holding the middle position between 4. Wanaheim and 6. Jötunheim, between 3. Asaheim and 7. Darkalf-world, between 2. Alfheim and 8. Helheim, and finally between 1. Muspellsheim and 9. Niflheim. But now, according to how the self conducts itself in life, whether the spiritual soul or the human soul overcame the other, the spirit itself will show the way — as its own judge of the dead [*Totenrichter*] for the disembodied soul — toward either Wanaheim or Jötunheim, i.e. toward higher spiritualization or toward lower materialization. This is neither reward nor punishment, but rather *Garma*, conditioned by the self's own will.

As the now disembodied self enters into a circle of spiritual forces — be this in Wanaheim or Jötunheim — it takes on those spiritual energies corresponding to the desires, inclinations and habits which it used to form its ideas and its desired and willed goals as spiritual conceptions in its last physical life. If these desired and willed goals were truly and deeply directed toward spiritual things such as art, science, ethics, etc., the self in question moves on into Wanaheim and there it leads a joyous spiritual life in the circle of those blessed spirits into whose orbit it brought its desires and longings — for all illusion and hypocrisy remain with the soulless body in the grave — and these (often unfulfilled) longings and strivings which prevailed in the previous human life are intensified in those spheres. But if this desire, striving and longing was directed toward material pleasure, material possessions, money and property in the previous life, the disembodied self will find others like itself in Jötunheim. Its appetitive body increases, but the means by which this appetite can be quelled are missing and so the soul suffers the torment of longing and remains bound with a thousand chains to the corporeal world. Since, however, these divine abodes are not to the found outside our terrestrial plane of humanity as geographical or topographical areas, but rather they are situated in the midst of our world the blessed spirits hover around in their astral bodies in the vicinity of their loved ones left behind on earth as good spirits and carry out familiar interactions with loved ones in that the provide them with good, kind thoughts and give them comfort, while those unhappy spirits,(35) likewise in their astral bodies, seek to satisfy their appetites. They hold up in dens of inequity where those appetites are indulged which correspond to their longings, and they even temporarily, for shorter or longer periods of time, take possession of the physical bodies of weak selves in order to satisfy their lusts in the physical bodies of such selves— lusts which were at first so delicious, but which have now become curses. This is that spiritual phenomenon of disease which we call delirium,(36) but which would be far more accurately characterized as possession. Whoever occasionally visits certain places will be able to confirm the fact — otherwise inexplicable — that in that place there seems to be a rather strange *fluidium* in the air. This seizes him like a frenzy and involuntarily motivates him to actions and excesses, or at least tempts him in directions he would not normally entertain, and this frenzy leaves him again as soon as the *no longer breathes that air*, i.e. leaves the place in question.(37)

But gradually the astral body fades and after it evaporates the self commences its migration toward the next divine world, i.e. either to Asaheim or Darkalf-heim, whichever is necessary. There similar processes are undergone until the self sheds the body of life, i.e. that body which still connects it materially to the human world. Only then does the animalistic life really cease, but the appetites remain and increase the torments as they now become more difficult to satisfy, while the satisfaction of the appetites toward spiritual properties are eased considerably, and thus afford blessed joys. Still clothed with the appetitive body, burdened by the final bonds to humanity, the soul enters Alfheim, or Half-world, whichever is appropriate to its progress. Only completely free spirits make it to Muspellsheim, while on the other hand completely fettered spirits go to Niflheim. From neither of these two divine worlds is there any further return to the human world by way of rebirth. In both places spirits remain in a fully conscious state until creation is renewed in the next cycle. The one in blessed remembrance and spiritual enjoyment, the other in a condition of torment and regret. But it is not hopeless, for they too can look forward to salvation in the next cycle, yet they have to seek to make their way once more from below upwards through all the levels of matter, struggling upward to attain a future human level, which they will inevitably obtain, even if it is at the end of time and space!

The disembodied souls in the other planes are reborn and in fact they will be born into definite circles where they manifest their inclinations and can see their wishes fulfilled, attracting things of equivalent value to themselves and repelling things unlike themselves, all according to their desires and inclinations working much like an electrical current. But the stronger the bonds of longing that fetter the disembodied self to the material world are, the harder its ascension into the spiritual planes up above Wanaheim is, and the longer it takes to complete the passage to Alfheim, where the longing for reincarnation — despite all the spiritual joys felt in the realms above — can still be felt quite strongly. The self then does not cross the last threshold to Muspellsheim, but rather is caused to turn back to strive for renewed incarnation on the earth. So the soul returns to Asaheim if it is not able to shed the appetitive body completely; or to Svartalfheim, if it only perceives a limited spiritual longing, to clothe itself anew with the body of life. Thus the urge toward rebirth grows and the soul quickly hurries through Asaheim or Svartalfheim to enter into Wanaheim or Jötunheim where it will be provided with a new astral body in preparation for rebirth on the earth.

Now if the upper divine worlds and the three lower worlds provide the appetitive body, the life-body and the astral body in equal measure to the soul as it presses toward rebirth, the ones provided by the upper divine worlds are nevertheless the more perfect and more noble because the soul returning to human existence would have enjoyed a much higher preparation in the upper divine worlds than is possible in the more material divine planes. Also, a self returning out of the upper divine worlds is much more clear and self-assured, and conscious of its own divinity and therefore more or less in a position to guide its own rebirth into humanity and to chose its own parents— ones compatible with it and ones with whom it will have a favorable relationship. This is something that the deluded selves pressing forth out of the lower divine realms toward rebirth unconsciously leave to outer circumstances. The saying: "He was unfortunate in his choice of parents" rests upon the recognition of ancient folk-wisdom, even if it is — like all other genuine and ancient sayings — misunderstood and used in a nonsensical way. But only that self which has broken the cycle of rebirths and become a "free spirit" and who rests within God in Muspellsheim — only such a self has broken every bond which binds it to humanity, for it has shed the appetitive body whereby it has attained complete freedom. Of course, it can, as a matter of free will, return to earth in order to complete some special mission. But afterwards it directs its development — uninfluenced by appetite and desire, and simply fulfilled by its exalted mission — toward rebirth in a human body. This is done in complete spiritual clarity, conscious of self and God, and it is then born on the earth as a "god-man" distinguished by special characteristic circumstances. Those families into which such god-men are born can expect all sorts of good fortune; but the god-man himself has to fulfill his mission, even if he is not allowed to have immediate success, and he dies in his youth as a martyr. Both Armanism and Wuotanism call such god-men "sons of the sun." At the moment of conception the self enters the human plane and in the womb begins to construct its own physical body — the mask of his essence (personality) — after it has already begun the initial origins of the essence with the formation of the life-body as well as the astral body. But since the self had shed first its physical body, and then slowly all the other layers or bodies after its last death, and only brings with it the remnants of the appetitive body from its last incarnation into the new one, it also forfeited all personal or essential memories associated with these shells, and only the instincts from earlier incarnations remain as dark impulses to act in decisive ways on its further development in its renewed human body. This constitutes the innate "good or evil gifts" of the newborn. But those spiritual treasures the self brings along from the upper divine worlds are called "talents" or at a higher level— "genius."

These nine divine worlds are not to be conceived of as spatially defined extraterrestrial localities above or below the earth, although esoterically in terms of Armanism such images are used in a symbolic language. What is actually being conveyed by this imagery are spiritual-fluidic circles, whose guides are the very spiritual entities we call gods, angels, saints, etc. Additionally, each of these circles is once more a multi-une / multi-fidic poly-unity [viel-einig–vielspältige Viel-Einheit] appearing integrated with subordinate circles, while at the same time they are connected to greater spheres of power and higher rings of spirituality. All of these spiritual rings, or divine worlds, live and interweave among us on the human plane itself, just as the human plane exists and functions in the midst of the animal, vegetable and mineral realms, and just as humans influence these things, humanity is influenced by these spiritual circles— perhaps even guided by them.

But Wuotanism has other homes of spirits and of the dead which correspond to the Armanic ideas just outlined, if one knows how to interpret the meanings. Thus the Wal (i.e. the harvest of the dead) is divided between Wuotan and Freya; each receives one half; that is, Wuotan receives the disembodied soul and Freya the disensouled body. The manner in which Wuotan and Lady Saga prepare their souls for rebirth has already been discussed previously. But Wuotanism recognizes two realms of the dead: Thrudheim (corresponding to Armanic Wana-heim) and Walhall (corresponding to Armanic Alfheim). Additionally, there are Hel-heim nd Niflheim, while the intermediate links are lacking. Freya's realm of the dead, Volkwang is Manaheim, or Fridhof [court of peace = Friedhof 'cemetery'] itself. It is only a heroic death which enables one to enter Walhall. This too is correct from an Armanic perspective because the hero (i.e. one who is active in life) will only have a brief stay in Wanaheim and Asaheim, arriving quickly in Alfheim (Walhall) there to attain his perfection— at least as far as possible. Thralls [Knechte](38) remain for the longest time in Wanaheim (Thrudheim) and rush through the upper realms in the semi-intoxicated state, if they reach them at all, and are almost immediately reborn without having gained the advantages offered by the upper divine abodes. Those who die a "straw death" go to Hel-heim. This is mistakenly thought to refer to those who die of natural causes in their beds, but a "straw death" actually indicates a meaningless death after a uselessly wasted and pointless life. This gives the matter a whole different meaning. Those who dread a straw death were useless slackers, they contributed nothing to the development of the world, these were those "who were not hot and not cold, and who are therefore to be condemned." Thus they will come again in order to become either hot or cold— which their Garma will force them to do by their own self-created sufferings. However, those who go to Niflheim, into the Hall of Serpents and to Nidhöggr (Neidhagen [= envy-enclosure]) the swallower of corpses are the evil-ones who will not be reborn. This is because the corpse-swallower wastes their bodies, and thereby cuts off any possibility of their return. They remain in that place of terror until the renewal of the world to work themselves painstakingly back up out of the fixed material realm to the level of humanity and human dignity. During this time, however, they retain awareness of their previous humanity. These are those who have committed sin against the Holy Spirit, a sin which — according to Catholic dogma — even the pope is unable to forgive, despite his "power of the keys." The anthropoid apes, the manlike apes, constitute that serpentine hall of Nidhöggr, hence that desire of these bestial men to breed with human women. However, these hybrids are infertile due to the intervention of a higher will.(39)

However, as concerns the Wuotanistic promises regarding the life of the disembodied souls in the different divine realms, these are to be obtained in the next life in a human body after death and after the next rebirth, for the self which makes its way through the divine worlds in a conscious and un-benumbed state as far as Asaheim earns a reincarnation in renewed human form conditioned in such a way that in the renewed human life all of those promises will be fulfilled that are promised to the Einherjar in Walhall. Likewise in the next human life the promises for all of those who prepare their souls for their next reincarnation in other divine abodes will be fulfilled. They become thralls on the earth, i.e. people who are not spiritually free, and trudge along under their yokes gnashing their teeth, or they live a lowly Phaeacian life with a Hel-bound spirit until necessity turns them into either heroes or criminals and determines that the path of their souls goes either to the right toward Wanaheim, or to the toward Jötunheim. But no self is lost, no soul, not the most infinitesimally small atomic particle throughout all of its millions of years of evolution — for all, all without exception, will be integrated at the end of space and time into the Great Spirit of Salvation and become one with it in order to cultivate remembrance in the Great Contemplation as the All-One-Ego [*All-Ein-Ich*], until after this has been assimilated, brings about a new "Let there be!"

Only after all of this has been said does it become possible to render as conceivable the incomparably magnificent symbol of the Aryo-Germanic world-tree, Yggdrasil. Yet here too the name itself in its three-leveled reading should be made the basis of the interpretation.(40) The conceptual and proper name "Yggdrasil" is broken up into three *Ur*-words: *ig*, *dra* and *sil*, which have the following meanings according to the three levels governing the ordering of words:

I. Level of Arising: *ig* = "I" as creator, generator, provider (*uig*, *wig* =) sacrality [*Weihe*] – *dra* (*thri*, *dri*) = turning, generation · – *sil* (*sal*) = salvation (*drasil* = spinning, flickering fire, *Ur*-fire).

II. Level of Being: *ig* (*uig*, *wig*) = viking – *dra* = drag, carry – *sil* = law, column [*Säule*] – *drasil* = bearer, horse.

III. Level of Passing Away: *ig* = terror, death – *dra* = destiny (dragon) – *sil* = target [*Ziel*], end. (*Drasil* = wood).

From this are derived the three conceptual interpretations of the word and name *Yggdrasil* (*ig-dra-sil*):

I. "I, the creator, generating salvation."
II. "Bearer of the fight of the spirit," "War-tree" and "War-horse."
III. "The aim of the terror of destruction." "Wood of terror."

The world-ash *Yggdrasil* is the tree of life of the Aryan people (the Fifth Root Race), it describes their purpose in coming into being, their sacral fire.(41) However, this tree lives or evolves as something tantamount to the entirety of humanity, as we think of its existence and power, and thus it is the bearer of the struggle — iconically as the war-horse — of humanity. And finally it will become the "wood of terror" by which humanity shall pass away. It is also the wind-cold tree sung about in Wuotan's runic song.(42) And in this way the designation as "world-ash" is meaningful— for ash is the *Ur*-word *ask*, and in the three levels this means: 1. arising, 2. the ash [tree], and 3. ashes (remnants of fire). Thus the *Ur*-father of humanity is called Ask (arising) and *man-ask*, "the arisen man" or the "moon arisen" (he who has his origins on the moon) and is the origin of our conceptual term for mankind [*Mensch*].

The main sanctuary [*Halgadom*] of the gods, and their most holy stead, is near the world-ash, Yggdrasil, the best and greatest of all trees because its branches spread out over the whole world and reach up over the top of heaven. The tree has three roots: the first reaches up to the Ases, the second to the rime-thurses or frost-giants where *ginnungagap* once was, and the third root sinks down to Niflheim to the smoking kettle (Hvergelmir), i.e. to the ancient well of the primeval world where Nidhöggr (the one that crouches low, who foments envy), the giant serpent, gnaws on the root from below. At the second root, which reaches to the frost-giants, there exists the well of Mimir (memory), who each morning drinks from the Gjallarhorn (*gi* = give; *all* = all; *ar* = ☉; *horen* = to bring forth— i.e. "giving everything to the all which is produced by the divine sun") and thereby takes in wisdom, or cosmic knowledge, from this horn. At the first root is Urda's well, where the gods hold court. From this spring emerged the Norns, fate, which is also decided there. Every day the Norns take water out of Urda's well and sprinkle it — along with the loamy soil (loamy soil = living matter), from down below — on the ash tree so that its branches do not wither (rebirth). The water from this well is so holy that everything that goes into the well becomes white as an eggshell. The dew that falls from the ash is called *hunangsfall*, honey dew, and is the nourishment of bees. Two birds are fed in Urda's well and they are called swans (*suan* = solar ancestors, ascent of the spirit) and from these are descended all of the swans on the earth. In the branches of the ash there sits an eagle who knows many things and between its eyes sits a hawk called Vedfölnir (the one which flies highest). The squirrel Ratatöskr (the one who scurries around) runs continuously up and down between the eagle and Nidhöggr carrying words of contention back and forth between the two in order to foment conflict between them. Four hinds around among the branches of the ash grazing on its buds. In Hvergelmir under the third root in Niflheim, there are so many serpents (more worms than foolish ninnys can imagine) that no tongue can name them, so says the *Gylfaginning*.

Armanism considered this magnificent image(43) from two perspectives: one from that of the All in the great world (macrocosm) and on from that of the All in the small world (microcosm), since as has been repeatedly shown, the law of similitude [*Gleichartigkeit*] (analogy) is prevalent everywhere. That the world-tree soars up over heaven is self-evident since it is itself the All; but the tree of mankind also reaches far out above the earth, as the cosmology of the Aryo-Germanic peoples has shown. In Wuotanism the stars are thought of as golden fruits (hence the golden nuts on the Yule-tide tree). The clouds are seen as the leaves and branches from which the dew that feeds the bees falls down to earth. In a similar way the other symbols are conceived of as literal realities in Wuotanism. This is different in Armanism. The first of the three roots reaches to the gods, the spiritual rulers; the second to the giants, the material rulers; the third to the realm of transformation— the realm of death. Here again it is a matter of the primeval three: arising, becoming and transformation. The world-tree, just like the tree of humanity, encompasses spirit and matter, light and darkness, heaven and earth, gods and men, good and evil at the same time. At the first root is Urda's well, the origin of the causeless cause, and of the Garmic web spinning out of it (i.e. the chain of causality). For this reason it is said elsewhere that this root reaches not only to the gods, but to the true men (the god-men, the "newly integrated men" [*Neueinen*]). This means that the gods are the guides and judges of the world, and this is the role they also play within those men whose spirit is like that of the gods. Every day the tree is moistened by the white (i.e. holy) water from the well of arising, from spirit and matter (living water and living earth). Upon this water swim the holy swans who perceive the sun— the consciousness of the divine. The second root goes into the material world, but it is precisely there that the well of wisdom springs up — the burn (= well) of knowledge — to which Wuotan (the earth-spirit) himself goes and gives his eye as a pledge in order to be able to drink wisdom from it. "Do you know what that means?" asks the Vala in the Völuspa. And we answer, "Yes, we know!"

In the constant transformation from arising to becoming and out beyond this to passing away, to a new arising and a new becoming, in which Wuotan continues in an uninterrupted evolutionary process — just as the All (macrocosm) and every individual self (microcosm) consistently remains the same *ego* [*Ich*] — this ego was from the beginning of time bound inseparably and unalterably to certain spiritual and physical realities in a biune-bifidic biunity [*beideinig-zwiespältige Zwei-Einheit*]. Thus Wuotan appears before our eyes as the reflection of the All as an individual self: "He consecrates himself, consecrated to himself," he consecrates himself — as a self-sacrificer to himself as a self-sacrifice — to the passing away in order to arise anew. The nearer he feels to the point in time for this *passing away toward a new arising* — his death — the clearer the knowledge grows in him about the secret of life which is an eternal arising and passing away, a constant transformation, an eternal return [*ewige Wiederkehr*]— a life of constant cycle of being born and dying. This knowledge completely arises in him only at that twilight-moment in which he is sinking (dying) into the *Ur* out of which he will once more arise, and in this twilight-moment (death) he gives his eye as a

unattainably grand epistemology of the divine (theognosis) as well as the doctrine of the origin of the cosmos (cosmogony) and a knowledge of humanity (anthropognosis) based upon it, and therefore they were ultimately able to elaborate such overwhelmingly magnificent poetic images. The fall of their schools into ruins was necessitated by the brazen law of arising, becoming and transformation toward a new arising.(51) Their teaching was complete, they themselves had outlived it and decay set in. This decay was, however, merely a death and not a destruction and so according to the same natural laws, a rebirth has to follow this death, and so it will. **But this will be the rebirth of the same self [Ichheit] but in another, renewed, essence [Wesenheit].** This belongs to the future, and in this future we hope only for the best for the Aryo-Germanic world, whose apostles already walk among us.(52)

That these *Armanen* and *Semanen*, who were thoroughly schooled in a scientific manner, and who were also investigating, working and teaching in an equally scientific manner, also knew and practiced astrology is also conceivable with no additional evidence. This is true even if some of the attestations sound mythical. But it is just this mythic quality which is the best proof of the great antiquity of this science. Wuotan — it is said — is the Father of Ages; the twelve divine fortresses enumerated in the "Gríminismál" are the twelve signs of the Zodiac to which Wuotan's twelve month-names are linked, as these are in turn linked to the Twelve-Gods of the months themselves. The doubt as to whether Wuotanism or Armanism could have possessed within its Ase-doctrine such a great deal of knowledge about astronomy disappears in the face of the fact that the same things are testified to for a tribe which is called "the wisest of all the bards [Barden].(53) Jordanes often speaks of the great priestly learnedness of the Goths (*Hist.* ch. V) and among the kinds of knowledge which at the time were considered as belonging to theology he expressly counts "the teaching of the twelve signs of heaven and the course of the planets" (ch. XI [69]). The Goths knew 346 stars by their own names. In Iceland there lived a man who was so experienced in astronomy, both through what he had learned from books and his own observations, that the establishment of the Christian reckoning of years was based upon his findings. His name was Oddi and he lived around the year 1000. Later he was called Stjörnu-Oddi (Star-Oddi). The seven days of the week were named, as has been shown, after the Aryo-Germanic divinities, something that Jon Ogmundarson, the first bishop of Holar in Iceland (1105), reproved and he futilely banned these names "as evil remnants of heathen custom." No less important to them was the "sidereal," or great cosmic year (*Annus magnus*), known from those calculations which revealed to them that this Year always had its inception when all seven planets were found together at the same time in a single solar house (sign of the Zodiac). It is extremely instructive to examine the meaning of the mystical number patterns found in the *Edda* and elsewhere which, however, for the most part usually go unnoticed. One example of this will suffice for our present purposes, since we have already interpreted the simple numbers one through ten. But this one additional example deserves its own special study.

48

In the divine Eddic lay Grímnismál 23 the following strophe occurs:
"Five hundred gates and four times ten,
I think there are this many in Walhalla;
From each one march eight hundred Einherjar
When they come to battle the Wolf."
The calculation is simple: 500 + 4 x 10 x 800 = 432,000. If we consider that Wuotan is thought of as a god of time in this ring, then those 432,000 Einherjar indicate years, which is confirmed by one of the many interpretations of the name, i.e. *ein* = one, *her, har* = year, *riar* = generator, or "generated single years.." But what do the 432,000 years mean?

The interpretation based on our Aryo-Germanic traditions, which flow but sparingly, but which nevertheless supply all the information we ever need, would lead us too far astray here, and due to our limited space we recommend H. P. Blavatsky's *Secret Doctrine* which gives a summary of the most important numbers having to do with years in which the mystical number 4320 forms the basis.[54] We already saw above that numbers have a mystical meaning which are basically different from their values in arithmetic, and each of the individual concepts of the simple number-words symbolizes within itself the greatest secrets of nature. Whether one takes the Four separate from the others, or the Three unto itself, or both all together resulting in Seven, or all three together which gives the Nine, concepts always appear on the surface of images which indicate and explain the most holy and concealed processes in regularly circulating (periodic) segments of time (cycles). These processes make their very specific influences felt— even in the layers of time. These are influences which again come to be expressed in very specific numerical correspondences. These regularly recurring layers and cycles of time and events, similar to the earthly year, all of which also, like the seasons of the year, have their developmental segments that indicate arising, becoming, transforming and passing away to a new beginning are called "rings" and "circles" in the *Edda* and are connected to mystical numbers mystically concealed. But there is not enough space in this work to clarify all this and this line of argumentation would also in and of itself exceed the aim of our book. Therefore, these numbers relating to yearly cycles are given here according to H. P. Blavatsky: "Such a ring or circle (cycle) comprises 4320 years, and such a cycle came to an end in the year 1897; therefore there is now a new age coming into force, one which is installing a new form of development." A Kali-Yuga comprises 432,000 years and that is the same number that designated the number of *Einherjar* above and which corresponds to that which is usually referred to as an Aeon and therefore here indicates the Aeon of Wuotanism.(55) A Maha-Yuga, a great era, has 4,320,000 years and comprises a segment of creation. A Day of Brahma is indicated there as having 4,420,000,000 years and a Night of Brahma has the same length. This means that the length of time for creation (materialization of the spirit) is 4,320,000,000 years and the time for the dissolution of matter into spirit (Surtur) has the same duration before a new cycle begins. Taken together the Day and Night of Brahma take 8,640,000,000 years, and if this enormous number is multiplied by 365 we arrive at the number for the Year of Brahma expressed in terms of terrestrial years. And a Century of Brahma (311,040,000.000.000 terrestrial years) produces the magnificent time span called the Maha Kalpa or the Age of Brahma. From this series of enormous numbers, which are cited here according to H. P. Blavatsky, one more may be introduced which indicates the age of humanity up to the year 1910: The years of our reckoning of time stand at exactly 18,618,751 terrestrial years, while the cosmic development of our solar system began exactly 1,955,884,710 earth-years ago, and therefore 2,364,411,590 years will be needed before there will be a return into the *Ur*.

From these enormous numbers, which find expression in our solar system where the solar spirit — All-Father — is enthroned, everything goes into even higher regions. For as we said above, Wuotanism characterizes the solar spirit as All-Father, while Armanism shifts the idea of the All-Father to being a cosmic spirit far above the solar spirit, far above the central-star spirit in incalculable levels of quantity out into the most inconceivably magnificent heights, and characterizes it only as the *One* which has no name that human tongues can speak or that human minds are able to comprehend. In the mysteries this name is called the "lost master-word" or the "lost name," a name which the master is supposed to seek after, for this name would give him all the power of the divinity itself. The content of this name is, however, the vibrational law in the full volume of the septad up and down the scale without beginning and without end. If a master, in imitation of Wuotan the "transformer" [*wandler*] (not the "wanderer" [*wanderer*]), slowly but surely acquires knowledge through constant transformation (being born, living, dying, entering the primeval state, and being reborn), through constant pledging of his one eye in the cycle of immeasurable spans of time, and through all of this finds the lost name of the divinity, then he himself becomes the hawk that sits between the two eyes of the eagle, then he will no longer be reborn, for then he will have found the lost master-word, and then he himself will have become God.

But the "lost master-word" is also *incommunicable*. The one who has found it — and it has been found many times already! — cannot communicate it to any of his brothers, for each one must seek it for himself — each one along his own self-chosen path, for it is on this path he will find it. This is because it is inevitable for him to find it for he was sent forth with the expressed purpose of finding it.

If one surveys the great artistic construction of the Aryo-Germanic *Wihinei* and then unifies it into a sort of focused single ray, it will be surprising in its overwhelming simplicity— one that can be summarized in a few sentences which not only make it possible for each man, in every life-situation, and in every profession, to lead his life according to *Wihinei* but actually motivate him in this direction so that he will find the shortest transformative path to find the "lost master-word"— or his own divinity.

These few sentences are easily derived from the concepts surrounding the simple series of numbers which we discussed in some detail above and each of which results from each of the others conditioned by unconscious memory of numerous earlier incarnations. These sentences read:

1.

Recognize God in Thy Self, and Man in Thy Essence, work for the Recognition of this through Word and Example for others, but do not force this Recognition onto others.

2.

Recognize the All-One-Self [*All-Ein-Ichheit*] in Thyself and Thy fellow men; deal with others as Thou wishest they would want to deal with Thee.

3.

Do not neglect Thy Spirit for the sake of Thy Body, nor Thy Body for the sake of Thy Spirit, thus Thou shalt always remain in balance, in that each of these supports the other and the God within Thee holds the guiding hand.

4.

Always listen to and follow Thy inner Voice and do what it advises Thee to do, and thus wilt Thou always know what Thou hast to do and Thou wilt strive toward the Good and avoid Evil.

5.

Let not Thy Heart vacillate and trust in the God within more than in the advice of strangers, for Thou alone canst know what guides Thee toward Salvation, for Thou art Thine own Judge.

6.

Recognize Thy duties as a human being to aid other selves toward Rebirth, as Thy parents helped Thee to Rebirth; facilitate these reincarnated Selves in Thy children as much as possible, that they may reach their goals through good upbringing and education and avoid misusing or squandering the creative force entrusted to Thee.

7.

Recognize that Thou hast been born into a Ring, be this Ring the Family, Community, Folk, State, etc., in order to work for the benefit of this Ring. Fulfill this Duty in complete devotion, but also demand the rights guaranteed to Thee, so that the balance will never be disturbed.

8.

Respect the Law and Contracts, always be truthful and without guile.

9.

Preserve Thy dignity as a human being in small things and great; always be calm, cheerful and joyous; bear with patience and dignity the suffering that is placed upon Thee and be not arrogant in times of luck, enjoy whatever pleasures life offers Thee, for enjoyment is Thy right, but steadfastly renounce whatever withholds it from Thee, because it is occasioned by Thy self-created Garma by means of Thine own will.

10.

Let the God in Thee govern; be strict with Thyself, though not in an ascetic manner, but be kind to others without weakness, and await death in quiet dignity as Thy friend who is kindly bringing Thee to Thy further evolution, perfection and happiness Thou hast been striving for.

Only a little more remains to be said. The Armanic *Wihinei* knew neither dogmas nor commandments, it also did not support blind faith, but rather it required knowledge. What each person recognized as being true was made manifest in his life, and he delved further within where he became aware of his own revelation through intuitive recognition. For this reason the Aryo-Germanics were confident, calm and inclined toward the enjoyment of life, for they did not fear death, as they knew that it was merely a brief span of time — similar to an invigorating sleep during the night — meant to impart renewed life once more. They knew that they would be their own descendants. For this reason they established families and estates for, by preparing for the future, they were actually providing for themselves. Therefore they exercised loyalty and maintained this loyalty to the death, for they knew what they were creating for themselves through this loyalty both in the primeval state [*Urständ*] and in the next incarnate life. Ultimately it is for this reason that they held women and marriage in such high, divine reverence and issued such strict laws against mixed marriages and bastardization, since they also recognized that the strength of the race was founded only on its unity and purity.

Dark times have come, but in spite of this we have not yet reached a twilight of the gods [*Götterdämmerung*] and even today we have no reason for doubt-filled pessimism, for the *Wihinei* of the Aryo-Germanics is too deep — even if unconscious and latent — rooted in every Aryo-Germanic soul and it awaits only the call to awaken which will and must catch fire in order to instill the flame of inspiration in the Aryo-Germanic sensibility, when — to use an old skaldic formula — the right word rings out at the right time in the right place.

Vienna, Ostarmond 00001910

Guido List

52
Notes

1 See the Grimms' tale entitled "The Seven Ravens."
2 Guido von List Bücherei Nr. 1 *Das Geheimnis der Runen*, etc. [This was published in English translation as *The Secret of the Runes* (Rochester, Vermont: Destiny, 1988).]
3 This process is easily conceivable when, according to the law of similarity or analogy (more on which later), spirit is compared to steam; just as it becomes water by means of condensation (inhalation) and finally turns into ice, so too did spirit become matter by means of a similar kind of condensation; spirit and steam remained what they are, and have only changed their forms of appearance. This too is an example of the triad: spirit, soul, body as: steam, water, ice. Cf. Guido-von-List-Bücherei Nr. 3 *Rita der Ario-Germanen*, pp. 9-14.
4 The three primeval races; the younger race of giants in the Fourth Race (the Atlanteans), and the Fifth Race is the Aryans. The Right-Aryans are the remnants of the Fourth Race.
5 See the Guido-von-List-Bücherei Nr. 4: *Die Völkernamen Germaniens und deren Deutungen*.
6 Rings were not, as they are today, exchanged. This is because only the girl has the ring (vagina) to promise, which is the same as the ring "Dripper" (Draupnir), which was burned with Baldur (in the form of his wife, Nana), and from it an equally heavy ring "drips" every ninth night (month). This is the mysterium of impregnation, pregnancy and giving birth.
7 This is not derived from *brach, brac* = "would know," but rather from *barac* = "to generate fruits." This has been erroneously derived from *Brachfeld*, which does not exist in June.
8 *Om* (*mononom* = magical word or holy unpronounceable name) *om* = holy praise of God. Cf. the Brahmanic OAM— omen, omega, amen, etc.
9 The other half, the bodies which have lost their souls, fall to Freya, who gathers them to herself in Volkswang [*Folkvangr*]— more about this later.
[10 Quote from the *Poetic Edda*, "Grímnismál" stanza 7: *þar þau Óðinn oc Sága / drecca um alla daga, // glöð, ór gullum kerum* — which is more literally translated: "...there Odin and Saga drink for all the days, glad (they are), from golden cups."]
11 The left foot is the *hlenke fos*, i.e. guide [*lenke*] generation, that is to say— the phallus.
12 Fridhof and not *Friedhof* [cemetery, literally "peace-yard"]; Fri, Death, rules in this yard and not peace [*Friede*]. Freya as the goddess of death therefore is also called Fria. One prayer to her goes like this: "Those fruits and children which thou grantest in abundance, lofty goddess, thine alone is the right to give life and to take it." Here with the word life should only be understood the life of the body [*Leib*], not that of the soul or spirit, for these are conferred by Wuotan.
13 The name Wuotan also means Odem ["breath"].
14 Gibre-altar = Giver-all-generator (Gibralter).
[15 Quote from Snorri's *Edda*, ch. 31, *á hann er gott at heita í einvígi*.]
16 Compare: bud = being born; bloom = living; fruit = dying; seed = death; the seed lies in the earth just as the dead lie in their graves.
17 The three levels of the ether are arranged from the bottom to the top: 1) electricity, 2) magnetism, and 3) the mysterious radiations (radium, cathode, Röntgen [X], etc.). Here the direction for the investigation of the last two elements might be indicated.
[18 This is a play on the fact that the Old Norse word *áss* can mean either "a god" or a "pillar or beam of wood." But these my be two different and unrelated words.]
19 Concerning this there are more details in the pioneering works of Dr. Jörg Lanz von Liebenfels from Rodaun near Vienna. Especially his *Theozoologie*, Vienna Moderner Verlag 1905. [An English translation of this seminal work is available from Rûna-Raven Press.] See also his *Affenmenschen der Bibel* ["Ape-men of the Bible]

53

and *Die Theologie und die assyrischen Menschentiere* ["Theology and the Assyrian Man-beasts"] Berlin-Lichterfelde, Paul Zillmann 1907.

20 See the works of Dr. Lanz von Liebenfels.

[21 List has already analyzed this word as meaning that which from the primeval beginning (*Ur*) has been there (*da*).]

[22 This idea is well-supported in Germanic lore, see Stephen E. Flowers' "Is Sigurŏr Sigmundr *aptrborinn?*" in *Studia Germanica* (Rûna-Raven, 2000), pp. 29-45.]

23 Concerning this see the highly interesting studies by Jos. Ludwig Reimer in his valuable works: *Ein pangermanisches Deutschland* and *Grundzüge der Deutschen Wiedergeburt* (Leipzig: Türingische Verlags-anstalt, 1906-1907). Both important books can not be too strongly recommended to all racial politicians; they utilize the ethical foundation given here in politically practical ways, and thereby attest to the possibility of their practical employment.

24 *Die Kardinalfrage der Menschheit (Unsterblichkeitslehre)* by Privy Councilor and Professor Max Seiling (Munich-Parsing), Leipzig: Oswald Mutze, 1907.

[25 The Gobelins are a family which started dye works in 15th century France and later founded a company that became renowned for the manufacture of fine tapestries.]

[26 This tortured formula is translated from the original: *vielspältig-vieleinige Viel-Einheit*.]

[27 This tortured formula is translated from the original: *allspältig-alleinige All-Einheit*.]

28 Many more such triads are known in mythology and folklore, the most important are: Three-Ases, Three-Brothers, each with three colors, rocks, women, wives, siblings, half-years, chieftains, houses, heavens, high-seats, courts, treasures, kings, heads, vats, maidens, Marys, months, nights, pounds, gold, places or rest, blows, sisters, senses, staves, bulls, days, thurses (giants), thursic daughters, drinks, monsters, valkyries, winters, roots, etc.

29 Smell, sight, taste, feeling, hearing, understanding, temperament; seven which the breath (Wuotan) unifies in the voice and places under the rulership of language.

30 Just as an aside it might be mentioned that "|" is the sign of the masculine being, while "O" is that of the feminine; unified as ⊕ the two signs as One indicate the bisexual (androgynous) being of the creator and form the holy letter "M," which has been preserved in the majuscule Gothic alphabet.

31 So, in passing it might be mentioned that our signs of increase in mathematics: the addition or plus sign + and the multiplication sign x have their origins in this. The plus (addition) indicates increase by means of augmentation: father + son + grandson, etc. The multiplication sign, however, shows increase by father x mother x descendants. More about this later.

[32 List is either pandering to his sexually repressed readership or is uninformed about the widespread sexual cult among the early Germanic peoples.]

33 Vol. V of *Deutsche Wiedergeburt*.

[34 "Secret, concealed, secretive; comfortable, snug" in the usage of current German.]

35 These are the so-called elementary spirits.

36 Delirium [*Irrsinn*] is different from delusion [*Wahnsinn*]. The latter is the excess of unsatisfied desires whereby delusional conceptions are generated which create an imaginary reality around the afflicted person. This is done by one's own mind and not by an outside one, which is the case with delirium.

37 Emile Zola quite succinctly calls that *fluidium* in such places (he is speaking of an erotic theater performance): "suggestion of the flesh."

38 Those who do not act or think independently, but rather are moved by ideas of good and evil, are designated as thralls— motivated by what is understood as "herd-mentality."

39 See the writings of Jörg von Liebenfels already cited previously.

40 For more details on this see Guido-von-List-Bücherei Nr. 1 *The Secret of the Runes* pp. 53, 71 and 72-3 and Nr. 5 *Die Bilderschrift der Ario-Germanen.*

54
41 Compare: "The burning thorn-bush," Exodus 3.2.

42 Hávamál 139, Runatals-thattr 1.

43 Professor Director Frierich Fischbach in Wiesbaden has created an incomparably beautiful representation of Yggdrasil as a design for a Goblin tapestry shown in his work *Ursprung der Buchstaben aus Runen mit den Ornamenten des Feuerkultus* (Origin of the Letters of the Alphabet from Runes with the Ornaments of the Fire-Cult), a design which deserves to become widely known. His other works are also most enthusiastically recommended here: *Asgart und Mittgart, nebst mythologische Flurkante* (Asgard and Midgard, along with other Mythological Landscapes), *Die schönsten Lieder der Edda* (The Most Beautiful Songs of the Edda), *Beiträge zur altgermanischen Mythologie* (Contributions on Old Germanic Mythology), etc., Verlag L. A. Kittler in Leipzig.

44 Mimir, Mime = Increasing reminder [*mehrende Mahnen*], memory; hence "mime" = actor.

45 The mysterium of the all-arising, all-becoming, and all-passing away toward an all-renewal.

46 Freya as the goddess of death (Fria), who takes care of the soulless bodies in the graveyard [*Friedhof*] (Volkswang); therefore the physical memory is preserved with her, while Wuotan takes the spiritual memory into account.

47 Mimir's head = the main- or head-knowledge [*Hauptwissen*] concerning arising, becoming, transformation, renewal (18th rune). Mimir's drink, the questioning of the Wala and Mimir's head are the three levels (grades) of the mysteries through which Wuotan becomes wise. *Sapienti sat!*

48 A Logos is always spiritual; but the Demiurge is a soul, i.e. already materialized.

49 *Geweih* from *gewige* derived from *wic, weihan* = consecration, power, holy, struggle, etc. Here it has the sense of power, consecration, holy in reference to rebirth and the ends or points of the horns have a phallic meaning, since from them the holy dew drops which nourishes the bees (souls) and promotes rebirth.

50 Greco-Roman geographers and historians transmitted these designations to us with faulty forms as *Irmionen, Hermanen, Semanen,* etc., and just as erroneously they called them tribes rather than levels of society. The *Armanen* were the scientists, the priesthood and therefore the cradle of the Aryo-Germanic *Ur*-nobility.

51 Concerning this process see *Der Übergang vom Wuotanismus zum Christentum.*

52 See *Das pangermanische Deutschland* and *Grundzüge der germanischen Wiedergeburt* by Jos. Ludwig Reimer.

53 *Paene omnibus barbaris Gothi (sic!) sapientivres semper exiterunt Graicis, que paene consimiles* ["Wherefore the Goths have ever been wiser than other barbarians and were nearly like the Greeks..."]: Jordanes *History of the Goths* ch. V (40). [For whatever reason List has translated *omnibus barbaris* as "other bards."]

[54 See, for example, Blavatsky's *Secret Doctrine* II, p. 68ff.]

55 From the beginning of our aeon until today (1910) 5012 years have gone by, and this same aeon will therefore last another 425,988 years.

55

Glossary

There are a few words which List uses repeatedly in some special sense or meaning. These bear separate definitions and commentary.

Acht [akht]: See *hohe heimliche Acht*. *hohe heimliche Acht* high secret tribunal (eight) *Acht* (octave), but as which music on an *Acht* (octave) higher

All: The entire cosmos, which includes everything in the objecive universe. The ego *(Ich)* differentitiates itself from the All, but nevertheless comes to realize its place within it in a conscious manner.

Garma: List formed this word based on the Sanskrit word *karma*: "action," and linked it with the Old Norse name of the hound of the underworld, Garmr, mentioned in the *Poetic Edda* (Völuspá 44, 49, 58 and Grímnismál 44).

Halgadom: A sanctuary, temple.

Ich: the ego, literally the "I." Related to this is the *Ich-heit*"self," individuality, which is characterized as the individuality which transcends various incarnations. The word Ichheit is made up of the first person singllar pronoun, *ich*, with an abstrating suffix: *-heit*. This is contrased with the *Wesenheit*.

Ur [oor]: This is used as a noun by List to indicate the undifferentiated primal state of the universe. Used as a prefix *(Ur-)* in German it indicates the original or primeval state or level of being of something.

Wihinei [VEE-inn-eye]: This is the Listian term for esoteric religion. The first syllable of the word, *wih-* reflects the Proto-Germanic *wîh-* "sacred." On page 28 of the present study, List himself defines the term sussently as "the inward sanctification."

Wesenheit: This is the substance or essence, which List characterizes as the "personality," i.e. personhood, and contrasts this witht he *Ichheit*.